THE HYPE HANDBOOK

12 INDISPENSABLE SUCCESS SECRETS

FROM THE WORLD'S GREATEST PROPAGANDISTS,

SELF-PROMOTERS, CULT LEADERS,

MISCHIEF MAKERS, AND BOUNDARY BREAKERS

MICHAEL F. SCHEIN

New York Chicago San Francisco Athens London
Madrid Mexico City Milan New Delhi
Singapore Sydney Toronto

1 2 3 4 5 6 7 8 9   LCR   25 24 23 22 21 20

ISBN   978-1-260-47013-0
MHID   1-260-47013-X

e-ISBN   978-1-260-47014-7
e-MHID   1-260-47014-8

McGraw Hill books are available at special quantity discounts to use as premiums and sales promotions or for use in corporate training programs. To contact a representative, please visit the Contact Us pages at www.mhprofessional.com.

*To Hazel Bean, my favorite person
in the whole wide world.*

CONTENTS

CONTENTS

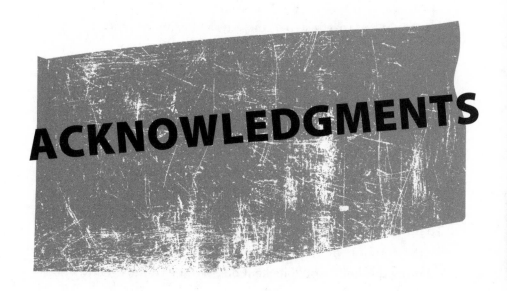

ACKNOWLEDGMENTS

I am fortunate to have many people in my life who I care about and who (I think) care about me. I originally set out to include them all in this section, but then I realized it would take up at least five pages. Plus, I'm pretty sure I'd still somehow manage to hurt someone's feelings by (unintentionally) leaving them out. So instead I decided to only include the small handful of people who directly impacted the creation of *The Hype Handbook*. If you're not on this list, it doesn't mean I don't love you . . . far from it.

Thank you . . .

To my agent, Heidi Krupp, who constantly astounds me with her ability to make big things happen.

To my editor, Donya Dickerson, who made this book better with every suggestion, while still always managing to protect my fragile writer's ego.

ACKNOWLEDGMENTS

To Corey Mead (and his amazing family, Laura Sims and Caleb "the Dragon" Sims-Mead) for reading multiple proposal drafts, encouraging me every step of the way, and being remarkably generous with his connections and time.

To Qingchi "C Bin" Bin and Zeyu Zheng, whose invitation to speak in Shenzhen on the topic of hype led to the publication of this book and so much more.

To Richard Laermer, who, over the course of countless dinners, schooled me in what it takes to make it as an author, speaker, marketer, and businessperson.

To my mom, Susan Schein, and my sister, Bonnie Schwartz (as well as the entire Schwartz clan—Jeremy, Emma, and Jolie), for believing this book would make it out into the world, even when I sometimes doubted it myself.

To the Beacon Writers Group, who reviewed an early draft at a pivotal time, which made all the difference.

To everyone on the McGraw Hill team.

And, of course, to Hazel Ray Schein, who is the reason I do everything.

INTRODUCTION

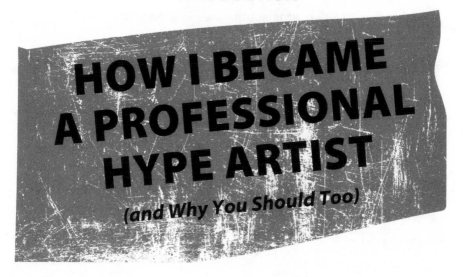

HOW I BECAME A PROFESSIONAL HYPE ARTIST
(and Why You Should Too)

Only in folklore does the world beat a path
to the inventor of a better mousetrap.

—RANDALL STROSS

When I was 34 years old, with a newborn baby at home, I decided I was going to ditch my cushy corporate career to make it on my own as a freelance writer.

Here's what I was thinking: Ever since I had circulated my hit story "WrestleMania 2230" in the second grade, people had been telling me I had talent. And when I left college, I really had tried to do something with my writing or at least in the arts: I interned at a television production company, wrote short stories, and started a band that built a following. But despite selling out a popular club on a weeknight, securing a residence there, and appearing on national TV (it was *Showtime at the Apollo* and we were booed offstage, but it still counts), I ultimately couldn't figure out how to support myself through my art.

So I got a job. The company that hired me operated customer service call centers. I told myself it was a temporary measure to provide some cash flow until I figured out what to do next.

I ended up working at that company for eight years—the better part of a decade. I learned a thing or two while I was there, but if I'm being honest with myself, the reasons I stayed for so long were the comfort my steadily increasing salary provided and my fear that I'd end up in a cardboard box if I left.

But then something happened that shook me out of my bubble-wrapped sleepwalk to the grave.

My wife got pregnant.

About three weeks after we got the news, I was lying in bed, and I had a vision. I saw my future child taking me to school for a Career Day event. I watched myself stand up and walk to the front of the class. I saw myself open my mouth and say the following words:

"Hi kids, I'm Michael Schein, and I'm Vice President of Solution Development at a business process outsourcing organization."

I quit my job three months later.

Fortunately I had a plan. I had read that big companies paid a few thousand dollars a pop for sales and marketing material written by good writers. I was a good writer. The way I saw it, if I could produce one of these bad boys a week, I could make the same amount of money I made at my job.

As you've probably guessed, my plan didn't work out as expected. I discovered pretty quick that being good at what you do isn't enough to get people to buy what you're selling. Our savings began to evaporate, and my wife began to ask questions about whether any of the handful of clients I managed to get were offering full-time work.

Instead of brushing up my résumé, I accelerated my hustle. I made cold calls all day. I went to networking events every evening. I wrote late into the night with my newborn perched on my chest. But when I looked at the numbers, we still weren't going to be able to keep this going for more than another six months.

I got depressed.

This was not how the major motion picture of my life was supposed to turn out. I had taken a risk. I had followed my dreams. I had pursued my gift. Why wasn't the promised worldly bounty following?

Then one afternoon I was walking to the subway after another unsuccessful sales meeting, and I passed that club my band had sold out years earlier. At first, the sight filled me with a new wave of self-loathing. Was my whole life one giant exercise in deluding myself? Even back then, what business did I have thinking I could make it as a musician? No one had ever said I was a good singer. I could barely play guitar. I had been a fool then, and I was a fool now. It was time to face the reality of mediocrity that I was destined to embody for the rest of my days.

But as I drew closer to the front door, I experienced a strange shift in my thinking. In my mind's eye, I saw that line of fans snaking around the building and through the front door—every one of them there to see us. And we had made that happen despite a lead singer with a nonexistent range and songs that everyone agreed would never get on the radio.

For the first time, it occurred to me that whatever success we had achieved was in spite of musical talent. I remembered how in our earliest days, we drummed up attention by posting flyers all over town that read, "Dave Matthews Must Die!" (sorry, Dave). How I built a following for us by walking the streets and taking the stage dressed as a nun. How we got press coverage by positioning ourselves as the "party band for the coming apocalypse."

Excitement began to well up in me for the first time in months. Maybe my real talent wasn't music—or even writing. Maybe I had more in common with the early rock managers who behaved more like outlaws than businesspeople than I did with the bands they represented.

Thinking back on it, I had always been enamored of those legendary promoters—poring over their stories in my younger days so I could apply the lessons I learned. There was Sex Pistols manager Malcolm McLaren who got England so agitated about the group that MPs brought it up in Parliament. There was Andrew Loog Oldham who came up with the saying, "Would you let your daughter go with a Rolling Stone?" There was Shep Gordon who turned the members of the original Alice Cooper Band into superstars by arranging for a truck to "accidentally" break down in the middle of London's Piccadilly Circus during rush hour while carrying a massive billboard of Alice himself, naked but for a boa constrictor draped over his nether regions.

Now facing failure, I once again thought back to this cavalcade of miscreants and what they represented.

There have always been people who operate on the fringes of respectable society. Rock bands and their managers, of course. But also medicine show men and circus hucksters and mentalists. Cult leaders and spiritual gurus. Propagandists and political agitators.

Since the standard wisdom about letting good work speak for itself, hustling hard, and implementing sales funnels wasn't doing me any good, I began to wonder whether there was anything in the strategies and techniques of these more unconventional operators that I could apply to my latest endeavor without losing my soul in the process.

THE STUDENT BECOMES A MASTER

It was at this point that I got a little obsessed. I read every biography I could find of history's most notoriously shameless self-promoters. Then I moved on to obscure sociology texts, books about crowd psychology, and esoteric tomes from past centuries. Next I uncovered the modern-day equivalents of these masters and interviewed them. I observed them in their natural habitat.

Then I decided to conduct an experiment.

One of the strategies I saw these characters using time and again in my research was what I now call "picking fights and making enemies." In short, they identify a person or a status quo idea and position themselves and their ideas in opposition to it. I had become convinced the tactic was effective.

And I already had the perfect target.

For those of you who aren't familiar with Gary Vaynerchuk, he's an internet marketer who made his name by preaching the gospel of hustle. In his books, videos, and talks, he constantly tells aspiring entrepreneurs that the only way to succeed is to spend the majority of every day talking about yourself online. For example, he talks about his habit of shooting tweets from the toilet at three in the morning as a healthy lifestyle choice.

His point of view had struck me as misguided for a long time—especially after I tried to put it into practice for myself and failed miserably. Now I finally screwed up the courage to say something about it. In an article I wrote on the subject, I publicly wondered why the only person who really seemed to be getting rich from the Vaynerchuk approach was Vaynerchuk himself. I posed the possibility that his advice was best suited for bolstering his own career rather than helping his followers bolster theirs. I presented the idea that a better strategy would be to stop paying attention to what he says to do and start modeling the mass psychology tactics he actually uses to turn young people into slavish acolytes.

My finger hovered over the mouse for a full 30 seconds before I clicked "Publish." Within an hour of posting the article, Gary Vaynerchuk himself recorded a video chewing me out by name. Vaynerchuk's horde of worshipful fans immediately began to berate me, calling me lazy, stupid, and jealous.

I got extremely nervous. I had really done it now. I had pissed off one of the biggest figures in the digital marketing space, and now I was paying the price. This was obviously my biggest blunder yet in the midst of a sea of whoppers.

But later that night I took a wayward look at my phone and saw something that blew me away. Over a period of 20 minutes, I gained a hundred new Twitter followers. I opened my email. My inbox was full of messages from people thanking me for saying what I had said because they had always felt the same way.

Within a week of publishing that article, I got my biggest client to date.

THE ART OF MORAL MANIPULATION

My initial experiment in benevolent mischief set off a snowball effect. Word got out about me beyond the initial fans of my contentious article, and potential clients started taking notice. Then potential clients became actual clients. Encouraged by the results, I ramped up my new approach. Before long, I had an unbroken flow of high-paying work. After a while, people began asking me how I had managed to do what I had done. Within a year of my big insight, my freelance writing practice had turned into a marketing agency.

It was the happy ending I had been looking for all along, and I should have felt unqualified joy. But I didn't. Something still bugged me about the secret knowledge I had uncovered. And I knew I had to do something to set my mind at ease.

Even though I had cracked some sort of code and was doing everything I could to apply my newfound knowledge to help make people's lives better, I was aware I was an unusual case. I understood that, on balance, the most malicious people among us tend to have the most intuitive understanding of these principles. At the same time, most well-meaning people fail to understand—or reject outright—these psychological realities.

As a result, harmful products, ideas, and ideologies tend to gain the most traction, while those that have the most potential to help people and move society forward often flounder.

It doesn't have to be this way. I had left my well-paying corporate job to try to make a difference in the world, but I knew that using my newfound understanding solely to grow my own client base was not enough. These principles had the potential to give an audience to the world's best ideas. To this end, I committed myself to spreading them wherever and whenever I could.

I grew up surrounded by opportunity, and the brush with financial instability I've described here is a fraction of the real long-term poverty so many in the world live with every day. That said, the experience did give me some small insight into what it really takes to break out and "make it" when you have limited resources.

It occurred to me that doing things the straightforward way is a privilege reserved for those with obvious options. It is no

accident that the promoters, propagandists, and various mischief makers I studied were so often outsiders when they started
out—whether by dint of poverty, class, or inclination. Driven by
the need to operate under the radar, they invented ingenious
workarounds that were designed to get the biggest results. These
people were, in essence, the original hackers.

It is a tradition that moves and mutates as time goes on and
surface-level details change but whose fundamentals remain relatively constant. Half a century after the heyday of the rock managers who inspired me, we see this dynamic play out in the dominant
cultural form of the twenty-first century.

Hip-hop is an art form that was originally created by young
people in some of the most economically disadvantaged neighbor-
hoods in America. Today its biggest star has a net worth of more
than a billion dollars. It should come as no surprise that the kind
of boundary-breaking self-promotion that conventional society
looks down on is celebrated in hip-hop in the form of the hype
man—a figure that exists for the sole purpose of drumming up
attention and excitement from the audience and on the streets.

It occurred to me that there is nothing inherently negative
about hype at all. In fact, during those times when life inevitably
backs us into a corner, perhaps hype is the secret door that could
provide the only way out.

WHAT IS HYPE, REALLY?

When people say that something is all hype, they usually mean
it's devoid of substance—a phenomenon that owes any attention
it gets to a crafty manipulator working behind the scenes to make
it look far more attractive than it really is. Hype is trivial. Hype is
distracting. Hype is empty. At its worst, hype is downright sinister.

But in reality, when handled with care, hype can be one of the most beneficial forces in existence. Hype is the practice of generating an intense emotional reaction from a large number of people to achieve a specific outcome. Cult leaders, propagandists, and other shameless self-promoters are naturals at this because they see human behavior more clearly than the rest of us. However, hype is not an inherently immoral force—it is simply a set of strategies, skills, and techniques. Throughout history it has been used to enable both creation and destruction.

According to common myths about success, making things happen requires iron will, single-minded vision, and tireless persistence. The truth is far more complicated. There have been many strong-willed, visionary go-getters whose ideas never made it past the walls of their huts. Bringing an idea to life requires hype. While the great inventors, engineers, scientists, and builders who worked on connecting the American coasts by locomotive and putting human beings on the moon should certainly get some credit, it was the hype artists who got people to show up and buy in that were truly indispensable.

With all of that said, there is a good reason hype has acquired such a bad reputation over the years. Sociopaths, narcissists, con artists, and other Machiavellian types are the most natural hype artists. They see the world through clearer eyes than the rest of us. However, this does not mean hype is innately immoral. Much like a gene seeking to reproduce, hype is amoral—a phenomenon altogether indifferent to societal notions of good and bad. And like biological evolution, hype is a creative force. Hype is not a mystical power, and it's not mass hypnosis or brainwashing. At the same time, it is not just another word for persuasion or sales. To be a hype artist is to interact with people based on how they really act rather than how they say—or think—they do.

For those of us who want to do right by people, and do what we can to make the world a little better, the trick is to selectively borrow those tactics and stunts from history's most effective attention-getters while leaving the unethical parts aside. Is this difficult? Sure it is. Is it worth it? Without a doubt.

Over the last few years, I've watched so many people with great ideas—ideas that could truly make the world a better place—fall short or get left behind because they didn't recognize the truth about what it takes to get the word out about what they were doing and get people whipped up into a frenzy about it. At my agency, MicroFame Media, our express purpose is to apply the principles of hype to draw attention to projects with big ideas we believe are improving people's lives. At a certain point, however, it began to dawn on me that even though I was proud of what my agency had accomplished for our clients, these strategies were too powerful to remain restricted to only those who happen to hire us.

Today success has become more dependent than ever before on the ability to mold perception. It became my mission to make sure those committed to making real contributions to the world have the same shot as those who are driven only by ruthless self-interest.

Setting this balance right is the reason I wrote the book you're holding in your hands.

The purpose of *The Hype Handbook* is to allow well-meaning people to achieve their personal and professional ambitions. The book provides a success template that readers can use no matter their temperament, budget, or background or even their level of natural ability. I've read hundreds of books, studied stacks of academic papers, and conducted countless interviews and experiments to get to the heart of what hype is all about and how it works. From this intensive study of the world's most effective boundary breakers and mischief makers, I have distilled 12 fundamental strategies that readers can use to bring into existence the reality they desire most.

A SNEAK PREVIEW

In the following pages, you'll hear stories of behind-the-scenes Svengalis who turned nobodies into superstars; obscure crackpots who got millions of people to buy into their ideas; and unknowns, freaks, and weirdos who garnered around-the-clock media attention without spending a penny. This book will serve as the bible for people who want to get known, get what they want, and get paid, and it is for everyone. At the same time, the lessons found in *The Hype Handbook* have particular relevance for Millennials and Generation Z readers. Members of these cohorts have learned the hard way that playing by society's rules doesn't work. Many of them watched their parents invest dutifully into retirement accounts only to have their savings wiped out by unscrupulous investment schemes. The straight-line path of college to job seems increasingly absurd to them in the face of crushing student debt. And their heroes have been, at various points, hackers like Steve Jobs, dropouts like Mark Zuckerberg, and former criminals like Jay-Z. They are looking for a realistic path to success and are unprecedented in their willingness to promote themselves.

Each chapter focuses on a principle of hype that I have drawn from the promoters and persuaders I have spent years studying and interacting with. It will be the go-to resource for anyone looking to get unstuck by generating excitement and moving people to action.

What you will discover is that all successful hype efforts share a finite number of characteristics. While each master of hype tends to lean most heavily on one tactic, or sometimes a handful, they all rely in some part on the full array of strategies I will describe.

In a perfect world, the best work would attract the most attention on its own merits. Unfortunately, it doesn't work that way. Instead, the single most important factor that determines whether something becomes a phenomenon or a flop is arguably the least understood—an ephemeral combination of manufactured drama, media manipulation, and behind-the-scenes maneuvering. By pinning down and organizing these principles, and presenting them in an easy-to-learn and easy-to-use format, I've attempted to make this magic formula accessible to the rest of us.

The human animal is not rational. We make decisions based on emotion and mental fallacies and then justify our choices afterward. So here's my message to you: If you are a business owner, entrepreneur, executive, artist, activist, or thinker who can honestly say that you are truly trying to make the world a better place, it is your moral imperative to learn how to harness raw emotion and irrational thinking to your benefit. You must come to understand how people really make decisions, why they really get excited, and why they really choose to follow some people over others. Then you must use your understanding of these principles for good.

To make this happen, study the mischief makers, the propagandists, the con artists, the boundary breakers, the hype artists. Find the commonalities. Reverse-engineer how they do what they do.

If certain people are able to reliably attract so many to useless products and sinister causes through the power of mischief and mass manipulation, imagine what could be done if more and more of us learned how to use these skills in the service of good. That's what this book is about. In an era where the line between spectacle and news is almost nonexistent, it is tempting to harken back to the myth of a golden age where reasoned discourse ruled the day and hype artists lurked shamefully in the shadows. The reality is far different. Hype is nothing new. It has, in fact—in one form or another—driven the course of human history since the time the first loinclothed scribe put reed to papyrus. Hype is as much a law of nature as natural selection. And like a gene seeking to reproduce, it is altogether indifferent to societal notions of good and evil.

It's true that Nazi propagandist Joseph Goebbels was a master at reframing commonly accepted reality. But then again, so was Martin Luther King Jr. While notorious con man "Dr." John R. Brinkley used spectacle to separate people from their hard-earned dollars, Richard Branson did the same. And while homicidal cult leader Jim Jones certainly knew how to foster feelings of transcendence, Mother Teresa made him look like an amateur. The book you hold in your hands takes the monopoly on hype away from the bad guys. It provides a blueprint the rest of us can use to move minds, get attention, and generate meaningful activity around our most cherished projects, businesses, causes, or works of art.

In short, *The Hype Handbook* shows you how to get everything you ever wanted without (necessarily) having to sell your soul. Read on to discover the secrets of how the human universe really works and how to use this newfound understanding to maximize the success of your business, your brand, or your bold new idea.

HYPE STRATEGY #1

MAKE WAR, NOT LOVE

Mass movements can rise and spread without belief
in a God but never without belief in a devil.
—ERIC HOFFER

Shep Gordon had a problem.

His client Alice Cooper had finally made it in America. Not only that, but Gordon had landed the band the gig of a lifetime—a headlining spot playing the 10,000-seat-capacity Wembley Arena in the United Kingdom. Unfortunately, the band had only managed to sell 500 of these seats, and there was less than a month before the big show.

Gordon had been in a similar spot before. When he had first started working with the Alice Cooper Band in Los Angeles, the mellow Southern California audiences hated the band's harsh garage rock sound. Never one to be deterred by something as unimportant as actual music, Gordon had pushed for the band to compensate with an increasingly theatrical live show. It wasn't long before an Alice Cooper performance looked a lot more like a circus freak tent than anything resembling a contemporary rock concert. However, the band wasn't translating overseas, and a failure on the scale of what was beginning to look inevitable as the Wembley show approached had the potential to upend all his hard work.

Lucky for him, pressure had always spurred Shep Gordon's best ideas.

A few days before the show, the manager secretly arranged to have a new promotional photo taken of Alice Cooper's lead singer. But this was no standard press shot. After a good deal of back-and-forth, Gordon convinced Alice Cooper to sprawl nude for the picture with only a boa constrictor covering his most sensitive area.

Next Gordon rented a truck, had the photo blown up to the size of a billboard, and had it mounted on the back of the vehicle. He found a driver who would be willing to risk a bit of jail time to take part in his plan and paid him handsomely to make it worth his while.

It was during rush hour that Shep Gordon lit the fuse on the hype bomb he had so meticulously prepared. The truck drove into the heart of Piccadilly Circus (the most highly trafficked area of London) and "broke down." London plunged into chaos. A line of cars snaked (no pun intended) for miles out of the heart of Piccadilly. News helicopters broadcast the image to households across the nation, sending respectable Brits into apoplectic fits. Parliament discussed banning the group from the country. Newspapers featured gems like "Ban Alice the Horror Rocker. He's Absolutely Sick." As for the kids—they loved it. Alice Cooper's newest single rocketed to the top of the UK charts. And Wembley Arena—the band sold out the entire venue, and Alice Cooper went on to become one of England's biggest acts.

HATRED: THE GREAT UNIFIER

From his earliest days as Alice Cooper's manager, Shep Gordon understood that trying to break the band solely on its sonic qualities gave them no advantage at all. The opportunity he saw was in positioning this band of weirdos as the embodiment of the generation gap that was at its height in the late sixties and early seventies. He reasoned that if he could get parents to see Alice Cooper as the antithesis of all the values they held dear, he would get hordes of their record-buying children to rally passionately around the band.

"I wanted to get all the parents in the world hating Alice Cooper," wrote Gordon in his autobiography, "and all the parents weren't reading *Rolling Stone* and *Creem*... We had to jump over the rock media and get Alice in *Newsweek* and *Time* and *Businessweek* and the newspapers and tabloids and evening news, all the places where the parents would see him and be revolted by him."

In the United States, the manager had made this happen by encouraging the members of the Alice Cooper Band to run with their most polarizing ideas. For example, their shows often featured mock executions, and they once took credit for the accidental dismemberment of a chicken at one of the their concerts. Parents were appalled, and kids couldn't get enough. Gordon's Piccadilly Circus plot in England was simply an extension of the same strategy.

WHY PICKING FIGHTS WORKS

There is nothing more effective for getting people to rally around a leader than the existence of a common enemy. While this doesn't mean you should go around calling on people to commit acts of violence or cruelty, you will need to publicly take a bold stand about what you're against, in addition to talking about what you're for. Shep Gordon instinctively knew what science has since confirmed. Human beings are driven to define themselves as part of an in-group, which they see as existing in contrast to some "other." In the case of Alice Cooper, that other was parents. The band members' antics earned them the outrage of moms and dads everywhere, which is exactly what made kids identify with them so strongly.

During a series of excavations of early human settlements on a promontory off the coast of South Africa called Pinnacle Point, anthropologist Curtis W. Marean developed a theory of why we are so strongly wired to interpret the world in this way. It was there that he uncovered evidence of habitation it would seem was the refuge of the remaining members of our species—a small handful of tribes—that were not wiped out during a mass extinction event. What kept the members of these tribes from going the way of the rest is that they uncovered a dense population of shellfish in the area. The only real impediment to getting their hands on that food source was the other tribes that were competing for it. Under these conditions, people who had a high propensity to cooperate with those they considered to be like them but to act aggressively to those they perceived were not tended to survive at a higher rate than others.

Once conditions improved, the descendants of these survivors spread to every corner of the globe. Their outlook is now encoded in our internal chemistry. For example, we form emotional attachments as a result of a neurotransmitter called oxytocin. When your brain secretes oxytocin in the presence of someone you are forming a relationship with, you experience a feeling of closeness, warmth, and commitment to that person. But oxytocin has another, lesser-known function as well. The same brain chemical that cements bonding with people inside your circle also causes you to experience feelings of hostility toward those outside your tribe. In other words, on a purely physical level, fomenting an us-versus-them dynamic creates stronger and stronger bonds between the leaders who spark divisions and those that follow them.

Our tribal tendencies may not be rational, but their pull is incredibly strong. If you're able to accept this facet of human nature, it places you in a powerful position. We live in a society that calls on us to relentlessly sell ourselves. But as the demands on us to self-promote grow more pressing, people are getting better and better at tuning out the self-serving messages they are bombarded with all day long. However, what our brains cannot disregard are messages that tell us to take sides. This is the secret the most effective hype artists understand. A hundred fifty thousand years and eight thousand miles away from the primal refuge where this behavior was born, it has continued to alter the course of world history.

THE CORNERSTONE OF PROPAGANDA

Regardless of whether you agree with the forty-fifth president's politics, there is no denying that the perception Trump has managed to create around himself is vastly at odds with the cold realities of his track record. After a few early high-profile real estate wins that were largely funded by his family fortune, his failures significantly outnumbered his successes. Trump

Steak. Trump Airlines. Trump Vodka. Trump Mortgage. *Trump Magazine.* Trump University. All were debacles—characterized by disappointed customers, stiffed vendors, and confusion on the part of virtually everyone involved.

The majority of businesspeople go out of their way to create great products, provide amazing service, and treat customers well. They do this based on the idea that each job well done will provide the foundation upon which to build the next win. When they do miss the mark, most of them work to repair the damage, make things right, and learn from the experience so they can create something more valuable and enduring the next time.

Trump is the exact opposite. He disregards the experience of his customers, partners, and vendors and any other data that might be telling him his latest venture is plummeting. Yet he is able to use each of his bombs to propel himself another step up the ladder because he is a natural hype artist, with a particular mastery of the skill we've been discussing in this chapter.

Here is an abbreviated list of the people and institutions that Trump has picked fights with since he became president: Mexicans, Muslims, Rosie O'Donnell, the continent of Africa, CNN, Megyn Kelly, NFL players, Omarosa Manigault, James Comey, Robert Mueller, Katy Tur, the cast of *Hamilton*, the Canadian Prime Minister, Harley-Davidson, Hunter Biden, Nancy Pelosi, NATO, and Greta Thunberg. The press and large swaths of social media spend a lot of time wringing their hands about this behavior. Yet the more the feuds he starts, the more his followers continue to adore him. Quite simply, the man has an intuitive understanding of human nature.

Trump's approach surprises many of us because it has, until now, been largely absent (or at least, not so overt) in American politics. But he is far from the first political figure in history to use this method. In fact, generating this sort of in-group versus out-group dynamic is a main feature of what is most commonly referred to as "propaganda." Social psychologists Elliot Aronson and Anthony Pratkanis have dedicated their careers to dissecting the propaganda techniques that the most successful leaders of mass movements have used to get large numbers of desperate people to identify with them, rally to their causes, and act according to how they would like them to act. In their landmark volume, *Age of Propaganda: The Everyday Use and Abuse of Persuasion,* they boil down the many tactics and techniques that propagandists use: "What the propagandist is really saying is 'You are on my side (never mind that I created the teams); now act like it and do what we say.'"

While some of the greatest tragedies in human history have been perpetuated as a result of propaganda, there is no denying that it works. While the content of what these propagandists promote may be evil, the mechanisms of mass persuasion they use are not tied to any specific morality. Picking a fight and creating us-versus-them dynamics can be as much about pitting new and interesting ideas against old and outmoded ones as it is about encouraging violence and hatred. As someone who is working to build attention and attraction around ideas that can make the world a better place (which I hope you are), it is essential to understand how human psychology really works rather than how we might wish it did. And few people understand this better than that subset of hype artists called propagandists.

So we must study them, learn what they know, and reapply their tactics for good. With that in mind, before moving on, we need to take a look at another of the masters of political propaganda whose strategies we can adapt and apply to whatever we happen to be working on.

NOT ALL ENEMIES ARE CREATED EQUAL

Otto von Bismarck was feeling frustrated. Despite having almost single-handedly transformed his country into a dominant European power as prime minister of the Kingdom of Prussia, the central mission of his life was still out of his grasp.

While Bismarck had been working to create a united German nation for years, the people of the 27 states of Central Europe were simply too far apart in terms of culture to consider joining together—especially with the militaristic Prussians at the helm. It was a problem for which he could not see a solution.

And then it hit him. He would start a war. Bismarck knew there was nothing quite like a war to unify people. But while he realized it was the answer he had been looking for, there was still one question remaining: Which enemy should he choose?

What Bismarck realized was that when it comes to driving a desired outcome, conflict can backfire as often as it succeeds. This master propagandist understood that in a population where many of the cultures, dialects, and perceived identities overlapped with those of the other nations that surrounded them, choosing the wrong enemy could divide the various German states further than they already were.

After a great deal of consideration. Otto von Bismarck settled on France.

The choice was an inspired one. All of the various German peoples had been raised on stories and legends about conflicts with their immediate non-German neighbor that stretched all the way back to Roman times.

Bismarck doctored a note that implied that the king of Prussia had insulted French dignitaries, and then he arranged for it to be published. When the French declared war in response, he was easily able to get the other German states to come to Prussia's defense.

After all, despite the differences the various Germans had with each other, those differences were nothing when compared with what the Germans felt about the aliens on the southwestern border.

The victory of the German alliance in this Franco-Prussian war engendered a newfound pride in the various states. It wasn't long before there was a brand-new country on the map—the unified nation of Germany.

Selecting the right enemy is key for any effective hype artist. But of all the potential conflicts out there, how do you make sure you're choosing the one that will result in the reaction you want members of your target audience to have?

In the Introduction, I described a pivotal incident in my early career in which I wrote an article about internet marketing guru Gary Vaynerchuk, taking him to task for his relentless focus on hustle. What made this small act of resistance resonate so widely was that so many others felt the same way but weren't speaking up about it. When they saw my article, they now had a way to put a structure around their beliefs and antagonisms.

Vaynerchuk's followers had long seen themselves as belonging to a tribe (they even call themselves "Vayniacs"). Now those outside the Vayniac circle who had read my piece had a way to identify themselves as another tribe that defined itself as being against the Vayniacs. And since every tribe needs a leader, and I was the one who stepped out first, I was able to easily assume that role.

The trick is to pinpoint a point of view that you've always disagreed with and that you strongly suspect a sizable number of others do too but aren't speaking up about. Are there business gurus out there that you believe are enriching themselves by giving bad advice? Take a public stand against them. Are there popular ideas floating around that you've long felt are absurd or harmful but that no one seems to be talking about? Be the one who does.

What you'll find is that when you take these sorts of bold positions, the many people who feel the same way you do will gather around you. And that's how movements are built. People follow other people with a point of view. Get one. Find a prominent figure in your field whose view you disagree with and point it out. Publicly. Repeatedly. And make sure you offer a viable alternative. If you can show people why a commonly held belief is causing more problems than it solves, they will come to see you as the leader of a new movement.

Does this mean that you need to continually insult and attack those who differ from you? Not necessarily. But it does mean you need to draw clear lines between yourself and others.

Ask yourself the following two questions: What point of view do you often encounter in your field that is so wrongheaded that it literally makes you angry? And what point of view in your field are you 100 percent, unshakably confident in? Get clear on your answers to these questions. Spend as long as you need to figure it out. Write your answers down on note cards and tape them above your desk.

Once you figure out the answers to these questions, they can serve as the nexus around which you build your tribe. Find people who differ from your point of view and challenge them on social media. Write articles disagreeing with commonly held orthodoxies in your industry. Pick fights with the gurus and thought leaders in your realm that have been around so long that no one thinks to challenge them anymore.

If you carve out a contrarian and challenging position, you will cause those who tend to see the world your way to rally around you and evangelize your ideas, even if others vehemently disagree with you. It's a strategy we encounter in all kinds of guises every day without realizing it. It was by using this strategy that Shep

Gordon turned the members of a garage rock band into mega-stars, Donald Trump got himself elected president, and Otto von Bismarck created a new nation. Steve Jobs positioned the Mac as a symbol of the new against the stodgy PC to bring the brand back from obsolescence. Original Rolling Stones manager Andrew Loog Oldham broke the blues band he managed by positioning it as the anti-Beatles with his brilliant catchphrase "Would you let your daughter go with a Rolling Stone?" The list goes on and on.

At the same time, this powerful strategy cannot exist on its own. If all you do is go around making enemies wherever you go, there will be no one to help you when you need it. Successful hype artists also cultivate relationships with great acumen.

Staking your career on the ability to pick fights while embracing personal connectivity is a paradox. It is how well you navigate this paradox that will ultimately determine your success.

Putting It into Practice

- Jot down a handful of opinions that you disagree with but that you regularly hear presented as gospel in your industry. This will form the basis of your contrarian point of view.
- Publicly call out a prominent guru whose opinion you disagree with. This is not the same thing as internet trolling. It is vital to focus on your object's point of view, rather than anything personal.
- Locate a heavily trafficked online community frequented by those in your desired audience. Here's where you can initially test your contrarian point of view. Once you get a strong reaction, move on to articles, videos, and talks.

CREATE YOUR OWN
SECRET SOCIETY
(the Piggybacking Principle)

The orator does not require to convert to his views all the members
of a jury, but only the leading spirits among it who will determine
the general opinion. As in all crowds, so in juries there are
a small number of individuals who serve as guides to the rest.

—GUSTAVE LE BON

While a plate of bacon and eggs is seen today as the quintessential American breakfast, this wasn't always the case. In fact, as recently as the early 1920s, most people in the United States kept their first meals of the day light. It wasn't until Edward Bernays set up shop as the original public relations professional that this all changed.

As nephew of psychiatrist Sigmund Freud, Edward Bernays was in a perfect position to learn about the inner workings of the human mind. However, Bernays lent his knowledge to purposes considerably less pure than those of his esteemed relative. Early in his career, Bernays worked as part of the Creel Committee—the propaganda agency responsible for selling World War I to the American public with sayings like "Make the World Safe for Democracy." He then turned his talents to the more lucrative private sector.

While on retainer to promote Lucky Strike cigarettes, he effectively eliminated the taboo of women smoking by organizing a "spontaneous" march in which suffragettes lit up cigarettes to demonstrate their liberation from the shackles of the past. He was behind a behind-the-scenes campaign to promote the idea that disposable cups were more sanitary than reusable ones on behalf of Dixie Cup. He even engineered the overthrow of a democratically elected government in Guatemala for the United Fruit Company.

It was while working on a campaign for Beech-Nut—one of the country's predominant producers of pork products at the time—that he managed to change the culinary patterns, and waistlines, of the American public forever after.

Edward Bernays had spent a great deal of his professional energy cultivating ties with some of the country's most influential people across various industries—people who themselves had webs of connections across their fields. Now he contacted a prominent physician and persuaded him to conduct a "study" on the health benefits of bacon. What the physician came back with was that bacon was, in fact, the perfect breakfast food in that it "replaces the energy you lose during sleep."

Once assured of these results, Bernays asked the doctor to communicate his findings to the medical community, which he did by distributing them to a list of 5,000 MDs across the United States. Within no time, doctors from coast to coast were recommending that their patients eat bacon for breakfast, and the dietary habits of a nation were transformed.

PIGGYBACK ON THOSE
WHO HAVE WHAT YOU WANT

Regardless of how you feel about the ethical implications of pushing packets of concentrated cholesterol on an unsuspecting public, there is a lot anyone selling anything can learn from Edward Bernays's notorious promotional campaign.

A lot of advice on marketing, promotion, and sales focuses on painstakingly building a following person by person. Bernays, on the other hand, understood that the appearance of a spontaneous grassroots following is far more important than whether it actually happens that way. Where he found real power was in identifying the individuals or institutions that had the most sway with the audiences and markets he needed to reach and then getting these individuals and institutions to want to advocate products, causes, messages, or ideas on his behalf.

It is difficult and time consuming to get masses of people to discover you and love you. The most effective hype artists hedge against this difficulty with a two-pronged approach. On one hand they generate the public perception of a spontaneous groundswell of dedicated attention (one of the best ways of doing this is detailed in the previous strategy). At the same time, however, they work assiduously to foster strategic alliances and mutually beneficial friendships. In many cases, it is the latter that has the biggest impact.

PLAYING WITH EGO, APPRECIATION, AND RECOGNITION

Before Andy Warhol became the legendary pop artist most people remember him as today, he was a kid named Andy Warhola from Pittsburgh who came to New York City to try to make it as a commercial illustrator. His earliest successes were in this field—providing him with the financial cushion to engage in the bold artistic experiments for which he eventually became known.

As a child of working-class immigrants, Warhol had no money and no connections. He compensated for these deficits by turning himself into a master of hype.

Whenever Warhol would show up at the office of a magazine or ad agency in his early career, he would present a little gift to the art director's receptionist. He would often bring coffee and doughnuts, run unsolicited errands, and pay lavish and sincere compliments to the power players most responsible for influencing his standing in their insular world. As he moved from the commercial to the fine art world, he used the same approach. While other artists were holed up in their studios painting, he made sure to put as much effort into socializing with, charming, and flattering the most influential gallery owners and curators of his day. And when he transitioned into filmmaking, he would go out of his way to arrange private screenings for the most influential critics in the independent film scene.

Warhol was certainly not above picking fights and provoking people. His paintings, his mass production methods, his look, his sexuality all made him enemies and got people worked up. However, what Warhol got—and what many notoriety seekers miss—is that while making waves in public is a great technique for generating publicity, it usually fails unless you lay the groundwork.

Beginning in 1969, Andy Warhol formalized and accelerated the technique that had always lain underneath his success. It was in this vein that he founded *Interview*—a magazine that, while much emulated since, was unique at the time in that it was entirely made up of interviews with celebrities, beautiful people, and tastemakers of various stripes. In addition to making the publication appealing in its own right, the format gave Warhol an excuse to connect with, talk to, and bond with the kinds of people who would inevitably boost his career. By the 1980s, the magazine was directly responsible for a steady stream of lucrative celebrity portrait commissions.

Warhol had always piggybacked on the success of people more powerful and influential than he was to accelerate his career. With *Interview*, he was simply doing the same thing on a larger scale.

The idea that success only comes to those who know important people is a fallacy. What hype artists understand is that while there are old boys' networks, circles of influence, and power centers, it is possible to break into them. How? By playing with the most deep-seated of human desires—to be recognized, to be appreciated, and to be noticed.

But the question still remains: Of all the people you could meet—of all the relationships you could massage (in the undoubtedly limited time you have in which to do so)—which ones should you choose?

FINDING THE RIGHT BACK TO PIGGY UPON

For the nine people left on the planet that don't know who Dr. Oz is, here's a recap. Mehmet Oz is a physician who, after focusing on practicing medicine for a few years, refashioned himself as a public personality. The career move went over well. *Time* dubbed him one of the 100 most influential people of the year. *Esquire* named him one of the 100 most influential people of the century. And in a demonstration of true editorial understatement, *Healthy Living* proclaimed him to be one of the greatest healers of the millennium.

But as Oz's fame grew, it became clear that healing was, in fact, not his only priority. In 2014, a team of medical researchers released a report proving that 60 percent of advice given on Dr. Oz's TV show lacked scientific basis. Soon afterward, 1,300 doctors signed an open letter calling him "a quack and a fake and a charlatan" whose "advice endangers patients."

Somehow the outcry did little to affect Dr. Oz's fortunes. His show won a Daytime Emmy in 2018. And later that year, the president of the United States appointed the good doctor to his council on sports, fitness, and nutrition. *The Dr. Oz Show* is still going strong. His net worth continues to soar, with a boost from his new role as spokesman for RealAge.com.

Having upward of a thousand people in your field publicly state that you were a fraud would sink many careers. So why is Dr. Oz still standing?

Above all, it comes down to one word:

Oprah.

Oprah Winfrey likes Dr. Oz. She helped create him. It was by appearing on her show that Oz got famous in the first place. Millions of people worship Oprah. They view her as a force of pure good in the universe. So when she continued to support Dr. Oz after his brush with disgrace, that was all many people needed to know. What was good enough for Oprah was good enough for them.

ALIGN YOURSELF WITH
THE MINI-OPRAHS OF YOUR WORLD

Here's the point where you might be asking yourself, "Did this guy seriously just recommend that I go out and meet Oprah Winfrey?"

Of course not. I understand that you are most probably not going to be able to get Oprah Winfrey to tout your wares. At the same time, there are undoubtedly mini-Oprahs in whatever niche you operate in.

One of the best parts of doing business in the age of the internet is that success doesn't require you to become well known and highly respected by everybody. You just have to become well known and highly respected in your niche. And these days, niches can get really specific.

Are you a corporate wellness coach for BPO professionals? Make a list of the mini-Oprahs in that space. A life coach who specializes in career transitions in the organic food industry? Find the mini-Oprahs. A consultant for north Alaskan salmon fisheries? You get the point.

Fortunately, it's a whole lot easier to get mini-Oprahs to know and like you than it is to do so with the real deal. One way to do this is to become a remarkably keen observer. Are there trade journalists in your field who get all the comments on the most relevant social media platforms? Are there admired gurus in your industry whose names are completely unfamiliar to your mother? These sorts of people will typically be far more responsive than full fledged celebrities, especially if you approach them the right way.

And what is the right way?

Once you've identified the people you need to know—and who need to like you—create (or adapt) a platform to showcase them. A mass celebrity like Oprah Winfrey needs to appear on major mass media to make it worth her while—network TV or satellite radio. A niche celebrity, on the other hand, will be content with niche media.

You're lucky to live in an era in which niche media is remarkably cheap and easy to produce. Blogs. Podcasts. Subreddits. YouTube channels. The specifics of the kind of online media that is relevant at the moment change all the time. Regardless of the specifics, the savviest digital-age micro-celebrities understand the value of appearing on lots of niche media outlets instead of (or in addition to) the old model of appearing on a handful of major media outlets. You can use their understanding to your benefit.

What you'll discover is that it often doesn't matter how new your platform is or whether anyone has ever heard of it. As long as you find ways to stroke the egos and show appreciation to the people you want to connect and bond with, they'll be incredibly receptive to appearing on it. Then, like Andy Warhol's *Interview*, you can use the conversation to kick off a relationship.

One way of harnessing ego and the desire to be appreciated and seen is to give your quarry a way to talk about a subject that means a lot to them and that they don't usually get to talk about. I remember hearing a story once about how in the seventies, when David Bowie was at the peak of his fame, it was almost impossible to get an in-depth interview with him, even for the most prominent journalists of the day. One young rock journalist from a minor publication decided to give it a shot anyway. He called Bowie's people, and they almost hung up on him. Fortunately for him, he managed to blurt out what he wanted to interview Bowie about before they did.

The saxophone.

You see, the saxophone was David Bowie's first instrument. He played it on every one of his albums. He loved the saxophone. Yet no one had ever thought to ask him about it. Sure, interviewers wanted to know about his songs. His singing. His costumes. His theatrics. His relationships. His debauchery. But never his sax playing.

Bowie's people knew about his love for the sax, even if the broader public didn't. And so they granted the interview. And while the interview began with questions about the superstar's woodwind prowess, it eventually went on to a wide range of topics, resulting in a fantastic in-depth piece and establishing the journalist's career.

Remember, the people you admire (and could benefit from knowing) are still human beings. They have needs, insecurities, and interests like everyone else. Dig into the crevices where others fear to tread.

Another way to create your secret circle of influence is to keep an eye out for people who will become the string-pullers of the future. Who are those wunderkinds who never stop, who are always impressing everyone, who always get things done? You know the types. The ultra-creative ones or the ultra-charismatic ones or the ultra-Machiavellian ones. Build your bond with them now before everyone is rushing to. By that time, it's often too late.

However, connecting with the members of your future secret cabal is no use if you don't do what you need to in order to hook them in and cement the bond. You need a circle of people who will be willing to do for you what Edward Bernays's doctor did for him.

BECOME THE PERSON
EVERYONE'S ALWAYS HAPPY TO HEAR FROM

When Chrissie Hynde wanted to get into the world of rock 'n' roll, moving from Akron, Ohio, to London, England, was only the beginning. In 1973, rock was a young man's game, and Hynde was an adult woman with no musical training. Yet within a few years she was fronting the Pretenders, a band that would eventually be inducted into the Rock and Roll Hall of Fame.

Chrissie Hynde's early success had little to do with the size of her mailing list or power of her elevator speech.

During an interview with Marc Maron on his *WTF* podcast, Hynde talked about how one of her first jobs in the UK was working at a clothing store owned by future music and fashion impresarios Malcolm McLaren and Vivienne Westwood. While Hynde was there, McLaren introduced her to a young man named John Lydon (Johnny Rotten), who would go on to front a band called the Sex Pistols. McLaren also connected her with David Johansen of the New York Dolls, which led to her first major gig.

At a certain point, Hynde introduced her old friend Johnny Rotten to Chris Spedding, another scenester she had met and who would ultimately record the Sex Pistols' first demos. When Hynde eventually started her own band, the Pretenders, and needed someone to architect its sound, Rotten connected her with legendary producer Chris Thomas.

And so on.

Although Hynde has stated that she "is the most hands-off businessperson in the history of the business," she has always instinctively grasped a key tenet of success that eludes many professionals: Reaching the pinnacle of your field is a function of getting to know the kind of people who can accelerate your growth in the shortest possible amount of time.

So how can you follow this literal rock star's example and use the power of relationships to electrify your own career?

Upon landing in London, Hynde jumped headfirst into the thriving music scene and impressed everyone who mattered with her in-depth knowledge and abiding love of rock 'n' roll. While social networks give unprecedented ability to connect with influencers, many businesspeople spend far too much time using these platforms to push their sales messages at the expense of forming real relationships. Instead of beating people over the head with industry-speak the first time you meet them, start with a conversation topic you both care deeply about. You'll be surprised how often getting to know someone over an area of mutual excitement leads to a remarkably meaningful bond.

In the early seventies, there was really only one role available for most women who wanted to be involved in the rock scene—the groupie. Groupies were known for collecting X-rated encounters with famous musicians and judged their "success" in terms of how many of these encounters they had. This was a game that Chrissie Hynde was not willing to play. Rather than aiming to put additional notches on her bedpost, Hynde went out of her way to build deep friendships with members of the scene she found interesting and talented. In turn, these friends helped her build her career.

The business world is not all that different. Plenty of networking "groupies," social and otherwise, spend their days collecting followers and business cards, only to wonder why these fleeting acquaintances fail to call them back the next day. Truly successful people, on the other hand, focus on the depth of their relationships.

Keep in mind that despite her ambition, Chrissie Hynde asked sparingly for favors from her friends. Instead, she looked for ways to help them—by introducing them to new bands, new musical ideas, and each other. As a result, rock's most influential people were always rooting for her to succeed and regularly volunteered to help her out.

Follow Chrissy Hynde's example. Introduce your newfound friends to each other. Offer to review their works in progress and share your ideas with them. The more generous you are, the more likely it is you'll have an army of influencers behind you helping to make you a star. But the idea here is not to be a networking whore who collects business cards at events and then fires off a bunch of random introductions every day. Your goal here is to be the man or woman that everyone important is happy to hear from when you call. You want to think depth, not breadth. The most influential "old boys' clubs" and secret societies don't accept everyone. And when you can't crack one that already exists, create your own. If you can do this, you have potentially unlimited power. Once you have this power, it's important to figure out what to do with it.

HOW TO USE THE SECRET SOCIETY YOU'VE BUILT

For years, Tucker Max, the author of *I Hope They Serve Beer in Hell*, was called "the king of fratire"—a guy best known for his stories of drunken womanizing. While this role was very lucrative for Mr. Max, certain changes in his life made him rethink his image. He now had a wife. A kid. The prospect of continuing to make his living as the patron saint of bro culture was no longer as appealing as it once was.

So Tucker Max decided to start a business. One that had nothing whatsoever to do with beer, babes, or partying. But it did have something to do with books. In fact, it was called Book in a Box—a service that businesspeople could use to quickly turn their ideas into an authority-building book. It was like ghostwriting on steroids.

There was only one problem: He had to build an audience—a customer base—around his new service, but none of the people who made up his current following associated him with anything other than debauchery. To start from scratch and build a new following around his new image would have taken years.

What he did instead was something that anyone aspiring to have a breakout book—or breakout business—should emulate. He contacted the various members of the tight clique of friends of which he was part. James Altucher, Ryan Holiday, Tim Ferriss, Lewis Howes. And he told them he had a new business venture he wanted the world to know about.

Max's friends immediately booked him on their podcasts, wrote about him on their blogs, and published articles about him—or rather, about Book in a Box. Within months, the company had generated $6 million worth of revenue.

Once you're sure the circle you've built around you is truly made up of your friends, and not just people in "your network," it's time to start pulling the behind-the-scenes levers of whatever really makes things happen in your world. What hype artists know is that secret cabals of powerful people who are helping each other out in the shadows really do exist. It was how Edward Bernays got America to eat bacon, how Andy Warhol got people to accept soup cans as art, and how Dr. Oz gets people to accept strawberries as a teeth whitener. And no matter where you come from, how much money you have, or who you know when you start out, it's a method available to you.

Putting It into Practice

- Launch a signature piece of media that is easy and inexpensive to produce and features interviews as its main event. Other people will be creating your content for you and will thank you for the opportunity.
- Make a list of people who have the power to help your career or introduce you to those who can. Find their contact information by doing an online or social media search. Invite them to take part in a podcast, webinar, or blog interview by telling them you're only talking with the top 50 people in the field.
- Host get-togethers. These can happen in person or virtually. Ask people in advance to come with a request for a piece of advice they want and with a favor they need. Be sure to bring your own as well.

PERFECT YOUR PACKAGING

The essence of propaganda is a well-designed package.

—ELLIOT ARONSON AND ANTHONY PRATKANIS

In the years immediately following World War I, a young German playwright decided communism was his thing. His name was Bertolt Brecht, and despite his attraction to radical equality, it was incredibly important to him that his name appear in lights. He realized, however, that his biting dramatic critiques of capitalism would lose all legitimacy the moment anyone discovered the real story of his upbringing.

Brecht came from a long line of businessmen, landowners, and white-collar professionals. Furthermore, the bookish young man had never done any of the sort of manual labor championed by the movement that had captured his imagination, and he had no intention of beginning to do so. Yet Brecht, every bit as talented a self-promoter as he was a playwright, saw in the Marxist vision of the world a terrific marketing opportunity.

After Germany's defeat in the war, the country's economic state was dire, and its mood was one of extreme humiliation. It was in this climate that the popularity of communism soared. The playwright seized the moment. Despite his crafting plays that were arty and intellectual, he constructed a persona that screamed *laborer*. He filled his wardrobe with the shirtsleeves and leather caps typically worn by mechanics and factory workers. He consistently sported a three-day stubble. He wore simple wire-rimmed "austerity spectacles."

Brecht was as concerned with dressing for success as any Fortune 500 CEO, and his view of how to do so was remarkably shrewd. He could have chosen to wear variations on the same kind of outfits that the other writers and thinkers in Weimar-era Germany favored. Instead, he used clothing as a mechanism to control how he was perceived. He had a certain image he knew was essential to his success, and he used what he wore to ensure this was the image people associated with him.

What made Brecht's strategy work so well for him was that he committed fully. He didn't only wear his worker's uniform on the opening night of a new play or in interviews but instead sported his signature garb at all times. In doing so, he became synonymous with the "working man's playwright." It's how people still think of him today.

Seventy years later, around the turn of the twenty-first century, a young American songwriter surveyed the music scene of the time and hated what he saw. Bro metal, rap rock, and vapid pop ruled the charts. Everything the young man had always loved about rock 'n' roll—the glamour, the flash, the artiness—seemed completely absent. To the young man, this was an egregious sin, and he set out to remedy it.

If you haven't guessed by now, that young man was me.

In 1999, I wrote a bunch of songs, assembled a group, and put together a stage show that would serve as a corrective to the times.

We had lights. We had confetti cannons. We convinced a friend to dance in a cage while wearing a gas mask. And we dressed awesome. Tight striped pants. Ascots. Pointy boots. Top hats.

It was a lot of work for a bunch of young scrappers, but we made it happen. We imagined the fantastical onstage world we had concocted to be the next in a line that included David Bowie, George Clinton, Devo, and even the musicals of Bertolt Brecht. We wrangled our first gig, called everyone we knew, and got them to call everyone they knew. We were convinced that when people saw our outrageous stage show and flamboyant outfits, word would spread throughout every corner of New York City and beyond.

That's not what happened. Even though the people we invited seemed to have a good time, the shows that followed were sparsely attended. As the months went on, it was clear the problem wasn't getting any better.

As a student of rock 'n' roll, I knew image was everything. As such, I figured if we dressed like rock legends on stage, we would become legends. What I failed to realize was that true rock stars have never drawn a distinction between stage and street.

I wasn't like that. My wardrobe was full of all kinds of clothing I had accumulated over the years during various phases of my life without much consideration. Khaki pants. Baggy jeans. Banker-blue button-down shirts. When I was onstage, I was a rock god.

In my day-to-day life, I chose what to wear by grabbing whatever happened to be clean.

Because the Lower East Side music scene was tight-knit, people undoubtedly noticed the contrast. As a result, my front man act came across as bogus. Even though we were putting on an entertaining show, we lacked the commitment to carry it through in the rest of our lives. We dressed for the moment but didn't use our clothing to tell a story. And that was where, at least in the beginning, we fell short.

TURNING YOUR INSIDES OUTWARD

One day I was complaining to one of my hippest friends about how we were failing to attain the heights of the rock legends we worshipped. She listened to me talk for about an hour. Then she looked me up and down.

"Do you really think Bowie would ever go out of the house looking like that?" she asked.

That was how, after playing a year's worth of sparsely attended shows, I filled a trash bag with all my khakis, button-downs, and functional shoes and hauled them down to the local Goodwill. It was then that I realized that if I was going to save rock 'n' roll, I should try to be a little better about living rock 'n' roll. From that day forward, I told myself that there would be no distinction between what I wore on stage and what I wore when walking around.

And you know what . . . it worked. We started to see the same faces at our shows again and again. Eventually we got a residency at the legendary New York venue Arlene's Grocery and then sold it out on a Wednesday night. We even recorded with the guys who had produced Sonic Youth and the Ramones.

Did we go on to play Madison Square Garden, hit number one on the charts, and embark on a decade-long sprint of decadence and debauchery? Nah. Turns out, it takes a lot more than clothing to drive rock 'n' roll stardom. That said, the strategy helped me—a third-rate guitar player who can barely sing—to get closer to being a rock star than I had any right to expect. And as I moved into the next phase of my career, the lessons I learned about how true stars in every field package themselves for success have stayed with me.

In traditional marketing, packaging refers to the wrapper you choose for the products you put on store shelves, with all the attendant color, texture, and font choices. As we've increasingly moved from a goods-based to service-based economy, considerations of packaging have grown to include things like visual brand identities and web design.

Master hype artists understand that focusing first on these sorts of details betrays a lack of understanding of the propagandistic power of packaging. They know that human beings are drawn to follow other human beings, rather than abstractions, and that the process by which they decide which other humans to follow operates on a primal, largely unconscious level. Since people can't crack open your skull and peer into your mind, they use the wrapping paper you choose for yourself to judge whether to follow or ignore you, without even realizing that's what they're doing.

Most professionals don't understand this. They view dressing for success as wearing a suit and tie to business meetings. Or maybe they don a blazer and new sneakers to show how creative they are, even though everyone around them is doing the same. As a result, they blend into the herd. Hype artists, on the other hand, draw on the deepest parts of themselves to construct a persona, often identifying and reworking parts that might come across as negative in other contexts. Then they commit to embodying this persona in every aspect of their lives and work.

Neil Strauss had risen to the pinnacle of his profession as a journalist, progressing from lowly intern to top ghostwriter for some of the biggest celebrities in the world. But he still wasn't happy. Why not? Because he was plagued by that unique combination of loneliness and shame that marks the romantically unsuccessful. Women simply didn't like him.

After a lifetime of being a romantic flop, Strauss had come to believe that people fell into one of two categories: naturally attractive people and naturally unattractive people. He was a member of the latter group, and there was nothing he could do about it.

But then he got a lead on an underground community of young men who had reverse-engineered how to successfully seduce women. He smelled a story, as well as an opportunity to improve the state of his own life.

Strauss infiltrated this community and immersed himself in its lifestyle. He attended a course on fixing his posture and took speech lessons to improve his "fast, quiet, and mumbly voice." After experimenting with cowboy hats, feather boas, and necklaces that lit up, he landed on a signature look of leather armbands, perfectly tailored shirts, and a shaved head.

Finally, he chose a new name that was better suited to his transformed identity—"Style." Before long, he was one of the most successful pickup artists in the world. The book that came out of the experience—*The Game: Penetrating the Secret Society of Pickup Artists*—would become a bestseller many times over.

The reason Strauss was so successful at reinventing himself in this way was that in the earliest days of his exploration, he happened upon a mentor who, it would quickly become clear, had an uncanny understanding of the psychology of attraction.

Mystery was a dark and charismatic figure instantly identifiable by his fuzzy top hat, layered jewelry, eyeliner, and painted black fingernails. When he entered a room, women's eyes floated in his direction before he ever said a word.

What the many imitators of Mystery who emerged in the wake of *The Game*'s publication failed to grasp was that his packaging was rooted in the core of who he was. Back when he was lonely Erik James Horvat-Markovic, he was already a fan of the theatrical, magical, and macabre in the form of Dungeons & Dragons. It was from that stereotypically unseductive starting place that he would go on to craft his eminently attractive persona. And attraction is simply another form of hype.

Neil Strauss ended up crafting his own packaging in a similar way. It is telling that Mystery gave him the nickname "Style" at one of their earliest meetings, well before Strauss had landed on his signature new look. As Strauss wrote, "That was one thing I prided myself on: I may never have been socially comfortable, but at least I knew how to dress better than those who were." His packaged persona was simply a consciously thought-out amplification of tendencies he already had.

Think Andy Warhol with his silver wig and foil-covered factory. Think Steve Jobs with his simple black turtlenecks or Ayn Rand with her black cape and dollar sign-shaped brooch pin. These master hype artists did not blend in, but neither did they package themselves haphazardly to court attention at all cost. True hype artists select each element of their external presentation to convey a specific message about who they are and what they can do.

The human brain did not evolve to give us an accurate view of reality. It evolved to help us survive and spread our genes. If we had to analyze and assess every one of the stimuli we encounter all day long, we would never be able to make decisions about anything. To accommodate this reality, our brains make constant predictions based on surface-level indicators similar to what has been encountered before. This processing happens instantaneously. The most effective hype artists understand this fundamental facet of human psychology and use it to their advantage.

Beginning in the first decades of the twentieth century, Kansas-based "Dr." John R. Brinkley developed a procedure he claimed could reinvigorate vitality and sexual potency in men. His procedure consisted of him cutting patients open and dropping goat testicles into their groin area. Over the course of his career, upward of 40 people died on the operating table or shortly afterward. Yet Brinkley was so popular that he became one of the richest and most famous inhabitants of his home state, at one point coming only a few votes shy of winning the governorship.

During Brinkley's heyday, there were plenty of other people hocking bogus miracle cures. However, most of these pitchmen carried with them the air of the circuses and medicine shows through which they had come up. Brinkley, on the other hand, positioned himself as more doctorly than even the most established physician. He unfailingly wore a white coat and the Vandyke beard that was associated with prestigious physicians at the time. He prominently displayed his medical school degree—one that he paid for and received in six weeks. He sprinkled his speech with medical terms and spoke with unfettered confidence at all times.

Gustave Le Bon, the social scientist who originated the discipline of crowd psychology in the late nineteenth century, once wrote that "prestige is the mainspring of all authority." Le Bon was not referring to accomplishment or talent or ability, all of which are rooted in the concrete and measurable. Prestige, on the other hand, is all about surfaces. It is about the symbols and signposts of leadership, success, and power. And if you are able to manipulate prestige to place yourself at the head of a tribe of those bound by mutual beliefs or mutual enemies, you can use that as the starting point to build a true movement.

It is important to expose people you wish to influence to indicators of your prestige as often as possible. If you once appeared on TV at two in the morning, there's no harm in placing "As Seen on CBS" on your website. If you once took out a tiny classified ad in the *New York Times*, you may want to allude to your appearance in the nation's paper of record. If people ask you about the details, certainly tell them. But what you'll find is that they usually don't.

SAME STUFF, DIFFERENT PACKAGE

Joe De Sena grew up in the largely Italian American neighborhood of Howard Beach in Queens, New York, in the 1970s. If you've ever seen the classic Martin Scorsese mobster flick *GoodFellas*, you're aware of the importance of processed meats, fried food, and the Catholic church in that neighborhood. So when De Sena's mother became a vegetarian yogi, it was not easy for him. Her transition made him and the rest of his family stick out, and it eventually contributed to his parents' divorce.

De Sena moved firmly in the other direction. He became a hard-hustling businessman. He turned gigs cleaning neighbors' pools into a full-fledged company. Then he went on to found a successful investment practice. His lifestyle became one defined by long hours behind a desk, little sleep, and nightly dinners full of rich food and wine.

Eventually, however, his lifestyle caught up with him. His energy faltered. His mood suffered. He felt sluggish and weak. He began to make bad decisions and fall short of his goals.

Many hard-driving people ignore these kinds of signs until they burn out (or have a heart attack). De Sena admits he would have done the same if not for the way he had grown up. "I would have been just like everybody else," he said. "We're all lemmings, and I would have done what everyone else does."

But unlike the other lemmings in his environment, this one had a mother who had transformed herself by radically shifting her physical and nutritional behaviors. For the first time in his life, he saw the value of what his hippie mom had figured out. Now instead of running from it, he embraced it.

De Sena was soon practicing yoga with the single-minded dedication he had applied to building his businesses. Before long, he was incorporating intense physical activity into every aspect of his life—from running up high-rise staircases to embarking on grueling wilderness treks. He put an end to the rich alcohol-fueled dinners and replaced them with raw food. He became obsessed with getting eight hours of sleep each night.

De Sena began persuading employees—and then clients—to embark on this lifestyle with him. Within a few years, spreading the word about this radically healthy way of living had become the most important thing in his world. For this purpose, De Sena started a second business called Peak, while still running his investment practice full-time.

As he saw it, the lifestyle he now practiced was so transformative that all he had to do was preach its benefits and the world would follow. He put whatever spare time he had—and spare cash—into the endeavor.

It failed.

A different person might have given up. After all, he had a successful finance business, and the new venture was draining his money and time. But De Sena understood the potential of his message to change lives, and he believed in it deeply. At the same time, he realized he was packaging that message all wrong.

In describing the shift that ultimately made his new venture a success, Joe De Sena explains, "I'm a snake oil salesman. I've had to deceive people and continue to deceive people. The reason is because human beings' number one source of motivation comes from avoiding discomfort." To counteract this ancient wiring, De Sena determined he needed to pinpoint a void that a large enough segment of modern people felt in their lives, and then he had to position what he was selling as the way to fill it.

To this end, De Sena figured out that a considerable number of people in the modern world felt unfulfilled by the soft lifestyle enabled by first-world countries. Armed with this knowledge, he developed a hypothesis that if he could give these people a common identity, he could override their reluctance to embark on the uncomfortable path of lifestyle change.

To make this happen, he reinvented Peak as Spartan Race.

At their core, Spartan Races are intense obstacle course challenges that test participants' strength and endurance at various levels. The courses emphasize commitment and strength, and they challenge you to stretch the limits of your capabilities. Everything is presented as an extension of the values of ancient Spartan culture—namely, those of self-reliance, physical perfection, and toughness.

It is the packaging that gives what he offers so much meaning to those who take part in it. It allows participants to see themselves as part of a 3,000-year-old tradition pioneered by a breed of warriors who dedicated their lives to personal betterment through rugged living.

"I think Spartan is really the yogi vegan thing wrapped in a cloak and an ancient Greek helmet," explains De Sena.

That the wrapping he chose is based on a hallowed tradition that has been memorialized in countless novels, works of art, and legends is no accident. Particularly after the release of the hit movie *300* in 2007, which depicts a stylized version of the Spartan victory against the Persians at Thermopylae, the designation of Spartan became synonymous in the popular imagination with toughness and tenacity and the ability to overcome obstacles. In other words, to be a "Spartan" has become prestigious.

From its start as a single race in Burlington, Vermont, in 2010, Spartan grew to 1 million racers participating in 250-plus events in more than 40 countries. There are also bestselling books, media productions, and community gatherings. Carola Jain, the company's chief marketing officer, describes it like this: "There are all these people—20,000 people—with Spartan tattoos. It's like a little cult. They want to go around and tell everybody because they know how positively it's impacted their life."

No matter what you're selling, there's a lot you can learn from Spartan Race's example. De Sena understood that when Aronson and Pratkanis are talking about the power of packaging, they are talking about something that—while it might be expressed visually—is fundamentally more profound. It is about how you use seemingly surface-level details to generate a cause, movement, or tribe in which people can invest their identities.

When you're deciding on your own package, consider what gap—of meaning or emotion or identity—you can help fill with what you produce. Then create a name, an image, and a message that people can latch onto and use to make themselves feel as if they are part of something vital and monumental. If you can do that, people will follow you anywhere you want to take them.

However, basing your packaging on a void in the marketplace—solely on what people want (whether or not they know it yet)—is not enough. Instead, you must find the spot where that void meets an image that only you and you alone can project and provide. What this means is that you need to figure out the inherent elements of your personality that make you *you*, your most treasured interests, and even your quirks and weaknesses.

Typically, we display these parts of ourselves in a haphazard and disjointed way, mixing our most revealing parts with those that society expects from us or that we just fall into. Work instead on eliminating those haphazard parts and replacing them with those that most accurately reflect the real you. Exaggerate these elements in your packaging. Blow them up. But whatever you do, don't bury them. Bring them to the fore.

Despite our modern so-called sophistication, we are every bit as tribal an animal as we were when our ancestors were scouring the Gold Coast of Africa for the shellfish that would save us from extinction. Ironically, human beings of all kinds are remarkably similar in most ways—from our genetic makeup to our behavioral patterns. What divides us is all surface level. As such, to lead people in the direction you want them to go, you need to take advantage of these manufactured divisions, and the only way to do so is to become a master of working with surfaces.

There is a reason chieftains and kings wore clothing that set them apart from the masses. There is a reason that national flags and symbols have, throughout history, exerted such a powerful sway over people that they have gone to war and died to defend them. We see these external pieces of packaging as inseparable from our identities.

Whenever you make a choice about the clothing you wear, the colors you display, the symbols (or logos) you use, think hard about how they can allow people to identify with a tribe or movement or type, which you lead and which the stuff you're selling embodies. Does it allow them to say, "I'm a Spartan," or "I'm a Communist," or "I'm a Vayniac" (or whatever the equivalent is in your case)? If so, you're on the right track.

Putting It into Practice

- Are there public figures from any era who embody the values, message, or identity you want people to associate with you? Begin collecting images of them. These are your style icons. Buy clothes that emulate what they were going for. Toss or donate the clothes in your wardrobe that don't fit your new image.
- Make a list of your quirks, most deeply held interests, and personality traits that have remained unchanged for as long as you can remember. Then brainstorm ways to reflect and embody these core traits and interests in your external presentation.
- Come up with a name for your followers and then refer to them by this constantly. It is not enough to collect anonymous followers on social media. You must tie them to each other by giving them a tribe to identify with.

GIVE THE LITTLE BABIES THEIR MILK

The bull gets inured to the plough by slow degrees.

—OVID

Life was hard in Paradise Valley.

Many of the residents of the Detroit neighborhood were African Americans who had migrated from the South in hopes of a better life courtesy of Ford Motors. However, by the 1930s it had already become clear to most who had made the move that an unofficial combination of inflated interest rates, discriminatory housing policies, and racial violence made social mobility every bit as difficult as it was in the land of sharecropping. It was Jim Crow with different packaging.

It was into this environment that Wallace D. Fard first emerged.

The first thing people noticed about him was how he dressed. In addition to his fine suits—a rarity in the impoverished neighborhood—he wore a Turkish-style fez perched upon his head. This, combined with his regal carriage, turned him into a walking conversation piece. It wasn't long before everyone in the neighborhood was wondering aloud what this mysterious stranger was all about. He was a splash of color in the middle of gray monotony.

Soon people started inviting Fard into their homes to attempt to satisfy their curiosity. It turned out he made his living as a salesman—one who trafficked in silk scarves imported from the East. Once a bit of small talk had ensued, Fard would spread the scarves before him on a table to discuss their quality and provenance.

The folks of Paradise Valley were a hospitable bunch, and at some point during their time together, someone would inevitably offer the merchant something to eat. It was at this point that Fard would proclaim that he followed strict dietary restrictions. In particular, he ate no pork and drank no alcohol.

In any African American community in the 1930s, this would have been considered very unusual. Even more than now, pork was a culinary staple. Yet as Fard talked about the benefits his lifestyle had bestowed upon him, his listeners' curiosity would grow. By the time the trim, dapper Fard left their home, many of the people he spoke with decided to give his strange diet a shot.

As in so many poor communities, the Detroit slums were characterized by poor health. Fatty pork products and excessive alcohol consumption led to problems like obesity, energy loss, and diabetes. So without fail, his customers' weight would drop, and their energy would increase. They came back to him amazed and excited.

It was only then that Fard would emphasize that these teachings came from his religion.

Wallace D. Fard was the founder of a new faith called the Nation of Islam (NOI). Its central doctrine was that an evil scientist named Yakub had created white people through genetic engineering. These pale-skinned beings were literal devils whose sole purpose was to destroy the utopia created by the original dark-skinned humans. Fard would inform his new associates that he practiced the purest form of Islam—a religion few African Americans in that period had ever encountered. In reality, the doctrine he preached had little to do with the ancient Middle Eastern faith from which Fard's religion derived its name.

Despite his apparent polish and cultivation, Fard had an extensive criminal record. Over the course of his life, he had taken on a wide variety of identities and had lived in many different locales. During his travels, he spent time dabbling in Freemasonry, the Theosophical Society, and the Moorish Science Temple of America. When he finally decided to make up his own religion, he picked out the most dazzling pieces of each of these philosophies, spiritual systems, and fraternal societies and cobbled them together.

Fard had no credentials or connections when he arrived in Paradise Valley. Yet a few months after coming to Detroit, he was regularly filling basements with excited people who wanted to hear him preach about his new religion.

Eventually the movement Fard wrought became a major cultural and political force. Much of this growth would ultimately take place under the subsequent leadership of his protégé Elijah Muhammad. And Muhammad's most effective evangelist was Malcolm Little—a charismatic ex-convict upon whom he bestowed the name Malcolm X.

When Muhammad first met Malcolm, he was impressed by the young man's passion. He also recognized that the flip side of this passion was that it caused Malcolm to fervently try to convince everyone he met of the righteousness of their cause with an intensity that often put people off.

After observing Malcolm's approach for some time, he called for the promising acolyte. Their meeting was short. The leader of the NOI sat Malcolm down and said only these simple words: "Give the little babies their milk before you give them their meat."

Malcolm understood. From that point on, he rarely mentioned the tenets of the Nation of Islam's theology—at least in his public talks. Instead, he spoke of the injustices African Americans had to deal with every day, along with the need for a new social and cultural structure that didn't position them as inherently less worthy than white people. It is probably no coincidence that the ministry of Malcolm X resulted in a 5,000 percent increase in conversions to the Nation of Islam within a few years.

The civil rights icon would abandon the Nation of Islam before his death, inspired by a pilgrimage to Mecca where he prayed side by side with people of all races. Other prominent figures like boxer Muhammad Ali and basketball player Kareem Abdul-Jabbar eventually left the NOI as well in order to adopt mainstream Islam.

Yet Fard's original vision lives on in some corners. When Elijah Muhammad's son disavowed the divisive elements of the NOI after his father's death and reestablished the group as the American Society of Muslims, a former calypso singer known as Louis Farrakhan broke from the parent organization and reestablished it under its original name. Relatively few people belong to his splinter sect, which many have pegged as a hate group. That said, Farrakhan is a master of the hype techniques pioneered by

Wallace D. Fard. As a result, he continues to get himself in the headlines year after year.

WHY MILK BEFORE MEAT WORKS

The founders of the Nation of Islam were not the first religious leaders to use the saying "Milk before meat" to explain the process of getting people to open up to, buy into, and then wholeheartedly embrace ideas that may have at one time seemed completely foreign or even truly distasteful to them.

In the Mormon Church's *Book of Doctrine and Covenants,* Jesus says to his followers that before they bring people news of his suffering on the cross, they should introduce them to simpler matters. "For they cannot bear meat now," he says, "but milk they must receive; wherefore, they must not know about these things, lest they perish."

When nineteenth-century celebrity preacher Henry Ward Beecher admitted to the feminist, free love advocate, and spiritualist Victoria Woodhull that he too aimed to help effect a change in the laws of marriage, she asked why he didn't preach those beliefs. His response was, "Milk for babies, meat for strong men."

Founders and early evangelists of new religions are faced with a formidable task. Even though we often come to accept the convoluted doctrines of world faiths once they become mainstream, almost all of them strike people as bizarre, even dangerous, when they first emerge. Yet some founders of new religions do manage to build massive followings around their belief systems, spawning legions of followers who transform the founders' beliefs into the new status quo.

What distinguishes these success stories from all the cults that (sometimes literally) go up in flames is how gradually the founders introduce their doctrines.

Kathleen Taylor, a cognitive scientist who studies the physiological basis of persuasion, writes that "Human brains are tuned for detecting changes, mismatches between their stored experiences and the information they are currently receiving . . . too big a gap between the ideas [influence technicians] hope to impose and those in present occupation of the target brain will lessen the chance of new ideas being accepted. Small steps, on the other hand, will be easier to swallow."

Stage magicians take advantage of this neurological quirk all the time. They will often distract members of the audience through onstage patter and visual deflection while slowly manipulating an object. Then when they redirect attention back to the original area, the change in position appears miraculous.

As a businessperson, you can take advantage of this aspect of our wiring to work magic of a different kind. New sales are the lifeblood of every business. The revenue they generate keeps a company running. For this reason, many of us push to get to the end of the sales process in as short a time as possible. The irony is that it is precisely this rush to close deals that often causes us to lose them.

The decision to part with a big chunk of money is the kind of change that terrified our prehistoric ancestors. To counteract this programming, focus on collecting small yeses instead.

In the old days when door-to-door salesmen prowled the land, the best of the herd concentrated on getting people to invite them into their homes rather than immediately getting them to open their wallets. In our own time, savvy online marketers concentrate the bulk of their efforts on getting prospects to download a piece of content in exchange for an email address rather than immediately asking for a credit card.

Follow their example. When you give your prospects a few sips of milk, it is only a matter time before they will be clamoring for the whole meal.

HOW TO DECIDE WHERE TO BEGIN

Hype, as we defined it earlier, is made up of two parts. To practice it effectively, you must engender an emotional reaction in people and get them to take action. Often, sparking emotion requires speed and suddenness. To get people to pay attention to you, you often have to set yourself apart like a diamond necklace against black felt. However, generating initial attraction does not inherently translate into influence. Lasting influence occurs in increments.

To determine which increment to introduce first, consider which piece of your message bears the most similarity to what people already understand, believe, or feel comfortable with.

A few decades after Jesus of Nazareth was crucified for preaching his radical new beliefs in Jerusalem, the movement he founded had plateaued. Followers of the Way (which is what Christianity was called back then) numbered in the dozens. But then, as every good Sunday school student knows, a zealous young Christian-hater named Saul of Tarsus, while on the road to Damascus, had a vision of the risen Jesus. Saul of Tarsus changed his name to Paul and became the most effective advocate for the new religion the world has ever known.

What is often not emphasized in the official version of this story is how entirely different the nascent Christian faith was when he encountered it from what it would become in his hands.

The earliest Christians—including the first apostles—thought of themselves as Jewish. They just happened to believe in the teachings of a new messiah. They kept kosher. They circumcised their sons. They didn't shave their faces. Most notably, they were only interested in spreading the teachings of their crucified leader to other Jewish people.

The soon-to-be Saint Paul changed all this. He alone got that there was a great deal of potential appeal in Jesus's teachings for the wider population of the Roman Empire. At the same time, he saw that very few people in the broader gladiator-loving population would be able to digest a comprehensive new spiritual system that contained ideas like "turning the other cheek" and the "meek inheriting the earth."

Paul solved this problem by packaging this radically new set of ideas in familiar wrapping paper and then introducing it to newcomers in gradual stages. For example, there is ample evidence that the original followers of Jesus did not emphasize the idea of salvation through Christ's blood on the cross. However, Paul had grown up in Tarsus—a city that was far more traditionally Roman than where Jesus and his followers were from.

It was in Tarsus that Paul undoubtedly experienced the popular ritual of the Mithraic cult, in which initiates drank wine to symbolize the blood of a sacred bull in order to gain admittance into its spiritual mysteries. It was also in Tarsus that he most likely encountered the story of Dionysus—a god who temporarily sheds his divinity so he can live among humanity.

The reason Paul was so successful in spreading his radical new faith in a way that would ultimately spread to every part of the planet is that he gave people what their culture and values could digest before he introduced everything else. It is also how the greatest civil rights legend in American history got two groups whose relations had always been characterized by distrust to come together to right one of history's great wrongs.

In the late 1950s and early 1960s, African Americans had every reason to hate the United States. A century after the Civil War, a war that was supposed to have freed them from servitude, they still lived under a system that enforced their status as decidedly inferior citizens.

It would have probably surprised nobody if Martin Luther King Jr. had used his speaking ability to disparage the nation, its system of government, and society as a whole.

Fortunately, King was too savvy for that. Instead, he co-opted the language of the institutions most dearly cherished by mainstream America. For example, in a notable sermon at the Ebenezer Baptist Church in 1965, King quoted entire passages of the Declaration of Independence. During the March on Washington, he referred to our "sweet land of liberty." And in the last speech of his life, he quoted the "Battle Hymn of the Republic" lyric: "Mine eyes have seen the glory of the coming of the Lord."

In an age where "disruption" is among the most common business buzzwords, many entrepreneurs lose sight of the fact that not everyone finds it so exhilarating to plunge into the great unknown. In fact, evolution has programmed most members of our species to fear large-scale change, even if that change would be good for us or for society.

Martin Luther King Jr. got around this by wrapping his message of intense change with the language and concepts of the trusted and familiar.

You should do the same.

In our professional lives, we often speak using the jargon of our own industries. We do this out of habit, and because it is efficient—at least when we're working with others in our own fields.

However, when we default to speaking in these terms to people we want to influence outside our fields—like potential customers—we often lose them. The way to combat this natural human tendency is to embark on the following exercise. It will only take a few minutes.

Take a piece of paper and draw a line down the center of the page. On the left, write down every technical term, acronym, and buzzword you and your colleagues regularly use. Then, on the right, next to each one of these terms, come up with a substitute that relates as directly as possible to the world the people in your intended audience inhabit.

Use this as your cheat sheet. Whenever the opportunity arises, practice communicating with the terms from the second column instead of the first. If you can train yourself to adopt the habit of cloaking the new ideas you wish people to adopt in the language they already use, your ability to influence them will dramatically increase.

MAKING IT THEIR IDEA

Question: What do Warren Buffett and Charles Manson have in common?

Answer: They were both star students of the Dale Carnegie training program.

The widely respected billionaire, sage, and investor Warren Buffett has famously claimed on multiple occasions that despite having attended Columbia Business School and the University of Nebraska, the only diploma he received that he was so proud of that he displayed it prominently on his wall was that from a Dale Carnegie Institute course, which he completed in 1952. To this day, Buffett maintains that the hundred-dollar fee he paid was the most valuable investment he ever made.

Only five years later, in 1957, a car thief and pimp named Charles Manson was doing a stint in a federal prison in California when he happened across a class the penitentiary was offering to inmates. The class was based on the book *How to Win Friends and Influence People* and lectures by the self-help author Dale Carnegie. The high school dropout dove into the coursework with a frenzy, becoming the top student in the program.

Dale Carnegie's work is all about communicating in a nonconfrontational way in order to massage people into seeing reality the way you want them to. One of his most powerful concepts is that of "letting the other fellow feel the idea is his." The central idea here is that one of the most effective ways of easing people into a desired course of action is to use words and framing that make it seem as if whatever you want them to do is originating from their own minds.

While Carnegie came to his insights largely through trial and error, subsequent science has confirmed many of his findings. In the mid-1960s, the husband and wife team of social psychologists Jack and Sharon Brehm demonstrated in a variety of experimental conditions that people would significantly alter their behavior, even to their own detriment, if they perceive that someone else is forcing them into undertaking that behavior.

Warren Buffett used his soft-handed approach to become one of the wealthiest people in history. Beneath the genial public persona for which he has become known is a shrewd player of interpersonal chess who almost always gets what he wants. As for Charles Manson, he used what he learned to infinitely more sinister ends.

It is often remarked upon with amazement that Manson was able to transform a group of nice middle-class kids into a cult of vicious murderers. It was the strain of the "milk before meat" strategy he first learned from Dale Carnegie that gave him this power.

When he spoke to Manson Family members, the leader would rarely tell them what to do—especially in the beginning of his relationship with them. Instead, he would regularly solicit his followers' advice, seizing on those instances when one of their partially formed ideas lined up with where he wanted them to go. Then he would subtly maneuver them—usually through questions—until the members of the Family were completely on board with the idea he favored.

Directly telling people what to do is the opposite of giving them milk before meat. The kind of slow and subtle questioning that Carnegie suggested is a far more powerful way to ease them into a point of view you want them to adopt—whether your aim in doing so is to create or to destroy.

In business, this is a strategy that extends far beyond sales—it is effective in leadership of all kinds. More times than not, when we tell people what we think they should do, they push back even if what you are recommending is in their best interest.

Whether you are trying to get a customer or client to buy something from you or get your team to go along with an idea you have that might be difficult or would require a great deal of work, replace every statement you would normally give as a command with a question.

Start by asking questions to get people to admit the challenges they are wrestling with. After that, ask questions to get them to unearth proposed solutions.

Those listening to you will inevitably propose a wide range of different ideas—many of which you don't really want them to land on. That's fine. When people propose solutions that don't get you to your desired end point, encourage them to give more ideas. However, when they finally land on a solution that is closer to where you want them to end up (and they inevitably will), seize on it and say, "That's a good idea! What else?"

Walk them through that journey, and eventually they'll come up with the idea you wanted them to come up with all along.

Often, we feel that in order to get people to do what we want, to take the actions we want them to take, we need to impose our will ever more strongly on them. If they don't listen to us, don't follow us, that's simply because we're not making our case forcefully enough. The best hype artists understand how foolish this is. They realize that once you've sparked attraction, the best way to get people to do what you want them to do is to have them get themselves there in steps so small that they don't even know it is happening.

Putting It into Practice

- Small yeses lead to successes. Often, when we engage in sales, we try to close the entire deal all at once and scare people off. Instead, decide in advance some small concession you can get your prospect to agree to.
- Break up large asks into micro-asks. Then put these micro-asks down on a calendar and follow the schedule to keep yourself disciplined.
- Ask questions. First probe to find out where the people you want to influence are struggling. Then ask additional questions to get them to propose potential solutions to their own problem. When you hear an idea that aligns with your agenda, seize on it. Agree and praise them for their great thinking.

BECOME A TRICKSTER
(at Least for a Little While)

One can get away with most anything by making people
tap their toes, laugh, or shake their heads in disbelief.

—KEMBREW MCLEOD

Only moments after the god Hermes was born, he snuck away
from his mother to do a prank. In this first day of his life, the
Greek god stole a herd of cattle from his elder half brother Apollo
and then set about inventing the lyre out of a tortoise shell. When
Apollo found out about his baby bro's antics, he was not pleased.
The elder deity was getting ready to take some Olympic-scale
revenge when Hermes proposed a deal. In exchange for Apollo's
forgiveness, Hermes would give him the lyre. Apollo couldn't help
but be amused by the little brat, took him up on his offer, and

became the god of music. As for Hermes, he became the god of thieves and would even go on to nab a spot on Mount Olympus.

Hermes is an example of a mythological figure that anthropologists call the "trickster." If you go back far enough, you'll find one in practically every culture in the world.

The Nez Perce tribe from what is now northeastern Idaho had Coyote who created traps for the purpose of fooling and confusing his fellow animal spirits. He eventually gave the traps to humans so they could catch fish and game and feed themselves. The Yoruba of western Africa had Eshu, a god who stole palm nuts from the monkey spirits and invented art. The Chinese told stories of the Monkey King, whose quick tongue made sure a Buddhist monk on pilgrimage arrived safely to his sacred destination. And the Scandinavians had Loki, a source of perpetual trouble and new ideas for Thor, Odin, and the rest of that gloomy northern bunch.

As Christianity replaced paganism, church fathers suppressed these myths, shoehorning aspects of the trickster gods into the figure of Satan. In doing this, they missed the point. While the devil is a figure of pure evil, tricksters are embodiments of mischief. And mischief plays a vital role in every society. In the words of the mythologist Lewis Hyde, "The Devil is an agent of evil, but trickster is *a*moral, not *im*moral."

It is easy for Olympians, kings and queens, and C-suite executives to look down on everyone else from their lofty positions and pass judgment on what is right and what is wrong. That's because they've already made it. But it's a different story when you're first starting out or doing something truly new. Or if circumstance has kept you from the advantages your competitors have.

We all come to our careers from different starting points. Some of us emerge into the business world with all the advantages, connections, and resources we need. Most of us don't. Using the tools of the trickster is often the only way for those of us who start off without advantages to catch up. Fortunately, if you choose to avail yourself of this brand of benevolent mischief, you can do so in a way that actually adds color to the lives of those around you.

"Where someone's sense of honorable behavior has left him unable to act," Lewis Hyde wrote, "trickster will appear to suggest an *a*moral [as opposed to *im*moral] action, something right/ wrong that will get life going again."

So what does it mean to become a trickster in the business world? How can you apply these tricks ethically while still advancing your interests?

How can you make them work for you if you don't come to it naturally?

As always, the answers to these questions can be found in the stories of those who have come before you.

INVERT NORMS

At the end of the nineteenth century, theater was the dominant form of live entertainment. Nowhere was that truer than in Paris. The French capital in 1897 had theaters of every size, in every part of the city. This made it tough for newcomers who wanted to enter the business, especially if they didn't have a lot of financial backing.

This was what made the proprietors of the Grand Guignol so remarkable. Founded in 1897 on a tiny budget by Oscar Méténier, and expanded and enhanced by Max Maurey, the Grand Guignol theater became one of Paris's must-visit destinations for the next 65 years.

The reason the Grand Guignol was able to thrive as so many of its competitors rose and fell around it: The two men behind its success were tricksters to the core.

When the tabloid journalist and marginal playwright Oscar Méténier decided he wanted to strike out on his own as an entrepreneur, he turned to the industry he knew best—the theater. However, past financial mismanagement limited his options when it came to finding a venue for his new venture. Not to be deterred, Méténier secured the only venue he could afford—an old church on a narrow back street.

Everything about Méténier's venue should have caused its failure. The church was small and cramped—by some accounts, the smallest playhouse in Paris. There was little separation between the audience and stage. The baroque religiosity of the decor had the potential to turn off theatergoers who were looking for a carefree, and often decadent, night on the town.

But, again, Méténier was a trickster. As such, he used every potentially off-putting element of his new theater to create an atmosphere of delicious disorientation, curiosity, and intrigue. Audience members sat in pews and in boxes that resembled confessional booths under Gothic vaulted ceilings with cherub gargoyles grinning down at them. Once people took their seats, they experienced an evening of plays unlike any others being performed in Paris—or anywhere else, for that matter.

The Grand Guignol featured plays drawn from the crime and depravity Méténier had witnessed during his time as a tabloid reporter. Few of the actual plays he or his successors produced there are remembered, and for good reason. As plays, they were not very good. Yet word spread quickly about this tiny venue on a tiny street.

Although France had already gone through its secular revolutions, the Catholic Church was still deeply embedded in the psyche of its citizens. By placing tales of sin in the context of a house of God, with all its accompanying accoutrements, Oscar Méténier created a fin de siècle version of a viral phenomenon.

Eventually Méténier sold the Grand Guignol to engineer-turned-entrepreneur Max Maurey. Even more commercially minded than his predecessor, Maurey ramped up the depravity. Under Maurey, an early proponent of special effects, the stage of the Grand Guignol featured blood spurting out of stab wounds, severed limbs, burning flesh, and decapitations.

Audiences were not prepared for what they saw, and it became common for members of the audience to faint during performances. Maurey took advantage of this. He made sure there was a doctor in attendance at every show. He leaked to the press a possibly apocryphal incident where a woman in the audience passed out, and her husband called for a doctor. Unfortunately, in this case, the doctor was not able to help because he too had fainted.

The Grand Guignol used a church—a symbol of goodness and cleanliness and piety—and transformed it into a venue for displays of humanity's basest impulses. It took the medium of Shakespeare and turned it into a gratuitous slaughterhouse. It took the healing arts and used them for a publicity stunt.

People often think that to stand out they need to do something entirely new. They feel that shock value for its own sake will get them the attention they crave. But often this approach backfires. Instead, it is by inverting norms that already exist that you create the appearance and sensation of novelty while still giving audiences the language and framework they need to allow themselves to let you in.

This was an approach Andrew Loog Oldham built his career on.

In 1964, the 19-year-old music manager didn't know what to do. While his band, the Rolling Stones, was getting a bit of traction, they seemed unable to break out as real stars. A big part of the problem was the Beatles. The Stones were good, but there didn't seem to be any room left for them.

The members of the Rolling Stones were middle-class boys with diverse backgrounds and tastes. Among the band's numbers was an alumnus of the United Kingdom's most prestigious business school, as well as a stately jazz drummer and a girl-shy guitarist with big ears. Lucky for everyone who loves rock music, Oldham had an idea that changed everything.

He gathered the bandmates and told them from then on they would play the role of "bad boys." Instead of trying to compete with the charming Beatles, who even grandmothers could tolerate, they would be rude, surly, and, by extension, dangerous whenever they interacted with the public.

Oldham was a trickster by inclination and necessity. He was raised by a single mother with no connections or money, and he was too young to be taken seriously by anyone who counted in the music business. Andrew Loog Oldham fashioned himself into a trickster because it was the only way for him to get from where he was to where he wanted to be.

The young manager took the standard image of the pop star prevalent at the time and turned it inside out. Where the Beatles—and the hordes of groups that followed in their wake—wore suits and ties, he encouraged the Stones to wear their grubby street clothes. Where the Beatles were polite to the television variety show hosts who invited them on, the Stones slouched and mumbled. Whereas the Beatles charmed the press, the Stones spit out rude answers to their questions.

In the words of *Rolling Stone* magazine reporter James Miller, "Oldham seduced the media, provoking them into saturation coverage of outrageous behavior (much of it either exaggerated or simply untrue)."

Even if you work in a more traditional industry than that of Méténier, Maurey, or Oldham, you can learn a lot from these tricksters.

Are there certain standards and assumptions in your industry or scene that everyone accepts as the way things are without questioning them? If so, write down every value, design element, system, way of thinking, belief, and any other piece that makes this entity what it is. Next, for each of these elements, think of its total opposite. Write those down as well.

For instance, take a virtually unquestioned maxim like "Hard work is essential to success." Is it possible there's an alternative to that worldview, such as "Successful people figure out how to work less hard and then convince unsuccessful people to work hard on their behalf"? (If you haven't figured it out by now, it was this exercise that led me to the public position I took that caused the fight with Gary Vaynerchuk that caused my career to take off.)

Ask yourself how you can embody these opposite elements in your packaging, your demeanor, and your public stance. It is there that you may find your winning pose.

MANUFACTURE MOMENTUM

When Macy's approached Marc Ecko and offered to give his hip-hop–influenced clothing line a try in one of its stores, he was both elated and terrified. He was elated because, well, it was Macy's. He was terrified because this single rack in a single store was his one and only chance to prove himself.

Ecko Unlimited knew there was a distinct possibility that customers would pass the rack by without buying a thing. He also knew that this would kill any momentum he had already built for his brand. He couldn't let that happen.

So what did he do? He contacted members of his street teams—kids he paid to plaster clubs and lampposts with the Ecko logo in various forms. Then he handed them some cash and told them, on the down low, to go into Macy's and buy his stuff.

The rack soon sold out. Macy's expanded its order. With a bigger blueprint in the store, non–street team members started purchasing Ecko clothing. In turn, Macy's expanded its order.

It was the beginning of an empire.

In remarking on his strategy years later, Marc Ecko said, "What's the takeaway here: Should you cheat to win? Yes and no. Long term, no, it'd be unscalable, unethical, and inauthentic to cook your books or buy your own inventory. That's bullshitting the world and bullshitting yourself. But when you're launching a business, and you believe in the fundamentals, think of it like a date; you want to make a good first impression."

Albert-László Barabási is a professor of network science who specializes in studying the effects of complex networks on performance. In 2018, he published a book called *The Formula: The Universal Laws of Success*, which was the culmination of a multiyear study in which he and his research team analyzed the common factors that a diverse range of successful people and projects share. What they found was that—more than quality or performance— success begets success: The factor that contributes the most to success is whether the person or project has already had success.

Fortunately, there are countless ways to manufacture momentum. Locate a small core of influential people who would be receptive to your product and provide them with all kinds of incentives to spread the word. Give them your product for free. Pump them up and make them feel like trendsetters. Hold a launch event, call on every friend you have to pack the room, and make sure people you know are on hand with some sort of camera or recording device to capture the crowds. When you spread the word—and the images—online, leave out the fact that this was a onetime occurrence. A few simple phrases—"another," "again," "our fans"—can create the perception that crowds like this one are the norm rather than the exception.

MAKE NEWS

The tricksters of myth had a knack for commanding attention from all the other gods that was disproportionate to the amount of actual power they had. For example, in Norse mythology, Loki was physically weaker than many of the other warlike deities of Asgard. Yet when he caused the death of Baldr the Bright—a being beloved by all the other gods for his beauty—by fooling the blind god Hodr into piercing Baldr with toxic mistletoe, the incident became the all-consuming obsession of all the gods. In other words, Loki generated news and caused it to spread.

It is a pattern many modern-day tricksters have followed.

Abbie Hoffman was a counterculture, antiwar protestor of the sixties variety who cofounded a new youth cultural movement he called the Yippies, which he positioned as the logical evolution from hippiedom. He organized a gathering in Washington, DC, where a crowd of self-proclaimed freaks attempted to levitate the Pentagon with their minds. He jumped up on stage during The

Who's set at Woodstock, only to receive a kick in the backside from guitarist Pete Townshend.

Each of these stunts garnered Hoffman and his movement massive amounts of press. Each of these stunts inspired imitators. Each of these stunts seemed like real news. And each of these stunts was concocted from the heads of Hoffman and his collaborators.

In describing his approach, Hoffman said, "If you don't like the news, why not go out and make your own?"

As the owner of a marketing agency, I get a lot of emails and calls from people who are looking to get attention for their businesses, products, and ideas. Most of these people are smart, and many of them are very accomplished. Yet when I ask them why journalists would want to feature them in their newspapers, magazines, TV shows, blogs, or podcasts, they usually launch into a description of all the wonderful features of their product, maybe with a little bit of history about their company thrown in.

It is important to keep in mind that journalists are not in the business of providing free advertising for products and services, regardless of how well made and useful they might be. Journalists are in the business of delivering news—or at least something that resembles news. If you want exposure for your stuff and for yourself, you need to follow Hoffman's advice.

Instead of taking out an ad for whatever you're selling, create and promote a holiday that celebrates its product category.

Rather than going from door to door to raise money for a charity, take inspiration from the ALS ice bucket challenge, which raised $115 million to fight amyotrophic lateral sclerosis (or Lou Gehrig's disease) by calling on people to post videos on social media of their friends and family dumping buckets of ice on their heads.

If you're an activist, follow the example of Pussy Riot.

In 2011, a group of Russian women who had become fed up with the accelerating authoritarianism and takeover of the media by President–Prime Minister–President Vladimir Putin created a gang of tricksters called Pussy Riot with the aim of combating the propagandist hype of their country's leader with street activist hype of their own. Not only did this group lack financial resources; it was largely barred from mass media outlets.

So the members of Pussy Riot asked themselves this question: "Where can we go to get in front of lots and lots of people with a message they won't be able to ignore, in a way that they won't be able to resist telling others?"

The answer they came up with: public transportation hubs.

Pussy Riot debuted its assault against the Russian status quo with a tour of Moscow's most heavily trafficked subway stations. The women donned trademark neon-bright face masks, plugged amplifiers into whatever source of electricity was closest by, and ripped into a cacophonous blast of sound and aggression.

In her book *Read & Riot: A Pussy Riot Guide to Activism*, Pussy Riot member Nadya Tolokonnikova described how the group ensured that news of these performances spread: "In the middle of a song, I would rip open a pillow and feathers would rain down on the subway station. . . . I would pull a large fire-cracker filled with multicolored confetti from my panties . . . and set it off. A layer of colored foil and paper covered stunned passengers who pressed the 'record' button on their phones and pointed them at us."

Pussy Riot created news and devised a mechanism for spreading that news that was embedded in their actual "product."

You may have no intention or desire to dress up, fight the power, or engage in public spectacle, but there is still a lot you can learn from this band of tricksters.

Begin by conducting an honest assessment. Are there people using your product in a way other than it was originally intended? Is there some sort of spectacle or event or dispute associated with what you produce? Is there a point of view that challenges the status quo that also has a tie to what you're selling? Is there a group of people who are inclined to use technology to capture what you do and share it with a wide audience? This is all the clay that the trickster digs up and molds to his or her own ends.

Once you figure this out, find the version of a public transit hub that's most applicable to you and your situation. In the digital age, this does not have to be a physical location. A well-trafficked subreddit? A particularly active YouTube comments section? A certain Quora answer section? Whatever it is, spend time there and display your own version of confetti pulled from underwear.

If you do this well, there will come a time when your tricks have gotten you to where you need to go and when you'll have to transition into a more prestigious role—to work your way into the circle of the Olympians. The question is, How do you know when that time has arrived?

MOVING BEYOND TRICKS

It was 2 a.m. and recent college dropout Ryan Holiday was defacing a billboard. The catch: The billboard was bought and paid for by Holiday and his client.

Holiday had recently dropped out of college to intern for Robert Greene—the Machiavellian master who authored such books as *The 48 Laws of Power* and *The Art of Seduction*—and then parlayed that experience into a web of connections with up-and-comers and the already-arrived like Tim Ferriss, James Altucher, and Tucker Max. It was on behalf of the last of these that Holiday would enact a campaign of tricksterism that would set off a firestorm.

The movie version of Tucker Max's controversial bestselling book *I Hope They Serve Beer in Hell* was about to come out, and Max had asked Holiday to help drum up attention for it. Despite the book's sales, Max and Holiday didn't have the kind of resources at their disposal that a large organization might. With the money they did have, Holiday and Max rented a small handful of billboards advertising the movie and then set about destroying them.

Holiday affixed on the billboard a message that made it clear that Tucker Max was a disgusting, woman-hating pig. The implication was that this message was placed there by a feminist who was so angry at Max and what he stood for that she was driven to vandalism.

Of course, the actual perpetrator made sure to take a picture of the newly defaced billboard. When he got home, he sent email under a bogus email account with a fake name to a handful of news and gossip blogs. Along with the attached photo, he wrote: "I saw these on my way home last night. It was on 3rd and Crescent Heights, I think. Good to know Los Angeles hates Tucker Max too."

News of the vandalism spread, and soon real feminists were defacing other Tucker Max billboards in emulation of their non-existent hero. Outrage skyrocketed. Woke college students picked up their picket signs to call for mass boycotts of the film. Major media outlets picked up on the furor, and pundits debated the merits of both sides.

Ticket sales soared.

These sorts of antics were Ryan Holiday's stock-in-trade for the early years of this precocious wunderkind's career. Barely out of his late teens, he secured a position as head of marketing for the clothing brand American Apparel. On its behalf, he used a tiny budget to secure porn star Sasha Grey for an ad where she wore nothing but socks (a naked girl for a clothing ad, get it?). He manufactured stories, pitched them to blogs, and got major media outlets to cover these stories as truth. He distributed antireligious messages on Christian websites and sexist messages on feminist websites—his only belief about any of the messages he spread having to do with whether they got covered or not.

Holiday's tactics were incredibly successful. They catapulted American Apparel into prominence (until the company eventually collapsed under a strange brew of paranoia, bad behavior, and poor decision-making by founder Dov Charney), and they made him one of the most coveted and emulated promoters around.

Holiday had other ambitions, though. Despite the crass humor and mischief of his tactics, his heroes were classical philosophers like Marcus Aurelius and Epictetus. He saw himself as a writer and a thinker and wanted to create great books that the public took seriously. Presumably he understood that his reputation as a trickster was not compatible with his achieving his larger goals.

It was with typical savvy that Ryan Holiday bridged the gap.

In 2012, Holiday published a book called *Trust Me, I'm Lying: Confessions of a Media Manipulator*. The book was billed as an exposé of the underhanded tricks that he had used to game the media and the gullible public. As evidenced by the fact that the alt-right eventually used this book (by Holiday's own admission) to move itself from the freakish fringe to the center of the cultural conversation, it makes no attempt to hide what some might call sinister and dishonest tactics from those who might use them for ill.

Holiday's real genius move was that he made it clear that buyers of the book will get their hands on these kinds of secrets, while he simultaneously used the book to begin to distance himself from the trickster image that would get in the way of the next phase of his career.

For example, a blurb on the back of *Trust Me, I'm Lying* reads: "Why am I giving away these secrets? Because I'm tired of a world where blogs take indirect bribes, marketers help write all the news, reckless journalists spread lies, and no one is accountable for any of it. I'm going to explain exactly how the media really works. What you choose to do with this information is up to you."

Brilliant.

The effectiveness of Holiday's distancing tactic is evident in what happened next. Among a number of other subsequent sober-minded books he put out, he released *The Obstacle Is the Way*, a reinterpretation of Stoic philosophy for the modern era. The audiobook version became incredibly popular among coaches and professional athletes, leading to his starting a web-based publication/business called *The Daily Stoic*, dedicated to promulgating the ideas of this philosophy of self-denial and moral fortitude.

Today Ryan Holiday's public image as a speaker and consultant, as well as that as a writer, is one of stern certainty. He speaks in unqualified terms about what his readers and followers should do to live upright lives in our decadent age. And people eat it up. He's bigger than ever.

His trickster past has been all but forgotten.

Being a trickster is extremely effective in the early stages of your career—or in the early stages of a new project or launch or initiative—especially when you're low on resources and obvious opportunities. For certain people in a limited range of fields— celebrity managers, shock jocks, and the like—being a lifelong trickster makes sense. For the rest of us, remaining a trickster can often become as much of a shackle as it once was a gate opener—

particularly when you're at that point when you want to move from the fringes to the centers of power.

The best hype artists know when to make this shift. They sense when to discredit their own past as an overt mischief maker and to embody an altogether new persona.

Putting It into Practice

- What are the standards and assumptions your industry accepts without question? Identify their opposites. Brainstorm ways to embody these counterintuitive ideas in your packaging, your demeanor, and your public stance.
- Manufacture momentum. Find people in your network who would be receptive to what you're selling. Give them your stuff for free. Provide incentives for them to spread the word online or at high-profile, real-life locations when you believe the most people will be paying attention.
- Once you've crossed from the fringes to the mainstream, start planning your shift away from mischief making.

BECOME
A MAGUS

Even the more reprehensible magicians have generally shown
a truer understanding of what constitutes human happiness
than most rulers and conquerors.

—E. M. BUTLER

Three thousand years ago, the land we now call Iran was ruled by a people called the Medes. The Medes organized themselves into six tribes, each of which was responsible for a different societal function. The first five are largely forgotten. The members of the sixth were called the magi.

The magi were the priests of the ancient Median civilization. Historians aren't certain about how they came to occupy the role, but what is clear from the archaeological record is the extent to which the Median kings depended on them.

Whenever a king was faced with a vital decision—such as whether or not to go to war—he would summon one of the magi for guidance. When called, the magus in question would—swathed in robes embroidered with strange symbols and bedecked in amulets and medallions—make his appearance. In exalted tones he would ask the king about the issue at hand.

Once this phase of the consultation was complete, the magus would withdraw. He would study the stars. He would draw up charts. He would recite incantations. He would confer with the gods.

After he had completed this extensive ritual, the magus would appear again before the king. With great ceremony, he would unveil a series of proclamations. The king would listen intently. Only then would he act.

This arrangement worked well for many years. Until it didn't. At some point, one of the long-subjugated groups of the Median Empire, the Persians, defeated their masters in battle and ended their reign. The Persian leader, Darius, declared himself king and embarked on the slaughter and enslavement of the vanquished ruling class, as was customary at the time.

Now you might think this would have been the end of the magi. Not only were they a powerful part of the Median aristocracy, but their forecast about the outcome of the most important battle in Iranian history up to that time was completely wrong.

But rather than getting themselves thrown into history's mass grave, the magi would somehow go on to maintain—and even increase—their influence as advisors under their new Persian rulers. Without so much as a battalion, they managed to conquer what would become one of the greatest military powers of all time.

In her 1947 book *The Myth of the Magus,* Cambridge professor Eliza Marian Butler held up the Median magi as the first known example of a type of figure that has amassed great power in virtually every civilization. This is the magician—a word that, in fact, takes its name from the magi of ancient Iran.

What is it, asked Butler, that has set the magician apart from other kinds of leaders and power brokers in a society? Her conclusion was that in order to cope with a world full of uncertainty, human beings have evolved a deep need for guidance from people they perceive as having access to the realm of the miraculous. Magicians, whatever they happen to call themselves in a particular era, satisfy this need.

But the question remains: How do human beings assess what experiences and phenomena are, in fact, miraculous?

Experimental psychologists Michael R. Ransom and Mark D. Alicke conducted a series of experiments in the year 2000 to determine the answer to precisely this question. The pair gave participants a string of scenarios describing improbable events— ranging from winning the lottery to recovering from a serious disease—but with slight variations in the specific details. Then the experimenters asked the subjects to indicate which of the scenarios were miracles and which were merely chance occurrences.

Of all the factors Ransom and Alicke observed, there were two that determined whether a subject saw a certain scenario as a miracle. One was the degree of surprise. For example, if the character in the scenario had found the winning lottery ticket on the sidewalk on a route they had never before taken to work, subjects tended to consider that more miraculous than someone who simply bought a ticket in a nearby deli.

The other main factor was "worthiness." In other words, if a child recovered from a terminal disease and then grew up to become a hero who saved a bunch of orphans from a burning building, subjects were more likely to see this as a miracle than if the child grew up to be an average Joe.

Ransom and Alicke called these signifiers "miracle heuristics." Despite what we might admit to ourselves, we have a deep need to believe in miracles as a way to find certainty and meaning. At the same time, we don't actually know how to distinguish miracles from that which is simply random and improbable. To resolve this tension, we subconsciously scan the landscape for easy-to-digest codes that tell us we're in the presence of the miraculous. Great hype artists understand this, and they use it. They deploy miracle heuristics to exploit the deep human attraction to magic in all its forms.

What follows are some specific ways true masters of hype manufacture miracle heuristics to attract attention, build fervent followings, and achieve outrageous objectives. Follow their lead, and you'll be able to do the same.

THE POWER OF MIRACULOUS FEATS

In 1987 Richard Branson, the founder of Virgin Records, received a call from a stranger named Per Lindstrand. It had occurred to Lindstrand, after having observed the exploits of the risk-taking entrepreneur in the press, that Branson would make an ideal partner in a venture Lindstrand had been planning for much of his adult life.

Lindstrand explained to Branson that no one had ever crossed the Atlantic in a hot-air balloon. There was a good reason for this. The kind of hot-air balloon that could withstand a journey of this duration would have to be massive, something that, as Branson would later describe it, "could swallow the Royal Albert Hall without showing a bulge." Because of the size required, however, the farthest anyone had ever flown one of these contraptions was 600 miles.

Unfortunately, to cross the Atlantic Ocean they would have to fly 3,000 miles. And if that weren't enough, the balloon would have to surf along violent wind currents as its main method of propulsion. The two of them would be all by themselves, with nothing but shark-infested waters below them and with no real method of backup if something should go wrong. Oh, and five people had already died trying to make the crossing.

Branson's reply was, "When do we start?"

Branson (along with Lindstrand) ended up traversing the 3,000 miles. Not only was this the most anyone had every traveled by that method, but it was the longest anyone had ever spent in a hot-air balloon. Before that the record was 27 hours, and he spent three times that amount of time in the air. He was almost killed on multiple occasions by tangled cables, dropped fueled tanks, and near drowning. At one point, his partner was lost at sea for a full hour.

Ultimately, however, Richard Branson, with Per Lindstrand, became the first person to ever cross the Atlantic in a hot-air balloon.

The reason I know about this story in such detail is because Richard Branson made sure of it. It was relentlessly covered in the media when it happened. He dedicated many pages to it in his bestselling autobiography *Losing My Virginity: How I Survived, Had Fun, and Made a Fortune Doing Business My Way*. And the description of how he undertook this perilous journey—and actually succeeded in making the crossing for the first time ever— has been told and retold countless times in retrospectives and "heroes-of-business" TV specials.

Still, there's one question I've never heard asked in any real way by any of the newscasters, cowriters, and television producers who have recounted this now legendary tale.

Why did Branson do it?

It's not as if Richard Branson had a lot of free time on his hands. Not only was he running a major record label; he was also in the midst of launching a new airline. It also wasn't as if he had a long deep-seated interest in hot-air ballooning. Until Lindstrand contacted him, he had never given it any thought at all. It is clear that Branson got a lot of publicity for the undertaking, but how did he know in advance it would be the right kind of publicity—the kind that would help Virgin make more money?

The real reason the entrepreneur-mogul sank so much time and effort into this perilous, impressive, and useless feat is that he is a master magician. The most successful magicians have always known that to deeply influence people it is not enough to simply point out miracles or even to make miracles—they have to *be* miracles. They understand that to get people to gravitate to them, they need to come across as the kid who grows up to become an uncommon hero rather than an average Joe.

It was with this understanding that the Theosophist guru Madame Helena Blavatsky actively spread rumors of her time between when she left Russia and came to America as one in which she had toured Serbia as a concert pianist and performed in a circus as a bareback horse rider. It was why "King" Benjamin Franklin Purnell, the founder of a turn-of-the-century religious cult called the House of David, led a baseball team that would regularly outscore its opponents by 25 to 30 runs. It was also why, closer to our own time, Kim Jong Il made sure that every time he played golf, the North Korean press reported that he hit 18 holes-in-one. And it's why Tim Ferriss's followers all know he takes baths full of ice, speaks 12 languages, and became a national kickboxing champion with record speed.

By crafting the persona of someone who has the ability to perform amazing feats, you tap into one of the two key miracle heuristics that Ransom and Alicke pinpointed—worthiness. And by choosing a feat that most people don't encounter every day, you tap into the other—surprise.

But the question still remains: If you don't have the stomach for death-defying stunts (or blatant lying), how can you tap into the power of miraculous feats?

HOW TO MAKE YOUR FEATS MIRACULOUS

Even if you aren't Richard Branson, you've had at least a few accomplishments over the course of your life. How do I know this about you? Because I've never met anyone who hasn't. You may think of them as no big deal or not much to talk about, but if you're a human being, you've got at least a handful of wins somewhere in your life story.

Despite what they'd have you believe, the number one difference between magicians like Branson and the rest of us is not the size and scope of their accomplishments. It's that they think and talk differently about those accomplishments. They have learned to present an easy-to-digest version of reality—one with a simple story arc in which they are protagonists using their powers to overcome clear-cut obstacles to achieve a worthy goal.

In interviews, when asked about her background, Ayn Rand would always give the same backstory. She fled to the United States from Russia in the wake of the Bolshevik Revolution. She came with no money. She had no connections. Yet through the force of her intellect and will, she was able to climb to the top of her field—first as a screenwriter and then as a bestselling novelist.

Of course, the full story was far more complicated. When Rand arrived in America, she was greeted by a large extended family that gave her a free place to stay and took great pains to make her feel comfortable. They also gave her loans, which allowed her to go to Hollywood and make her way in the screen trade. But Rand's glossing over all these nuances in her tale was no accident. The help her family provided simply didn't fit the persona of the ultimate free market capitalist on which she built her career, and for which she is still known today.

In telling your own story, whether it's in an interview, on a YouTube video, or at a dinner table full of important connections, don't leave the filter through which you present your accomplishments (no matter how minor they might seem to you) up to chance. Always start by asking yourself: "What's my persona?" and "What's my narrative arc?" If there's a detail that doesn't fit into one of these two buckets, think twice before bringing it up.

At the same time, there's a fine line between learning to tell your story in the most persuasive way possible and being a braggadocious liar. The latter will ultimately work against you because, despite appearances to the contrary, most people are surprisingly good at spotting truly blatant bunk.

To stay on the right side of this line, think of the various elements of your narrative as faders on a music studio mixing board. When recording engineers mix a track, they could theoretically place every instrument—bass, guitar, drums, vocals, and keyboards—at the same level. But this would make the result an ugly blob of noise, no matter how good the underlying song actually is. Instead, they raise and lower different instruments in the mix. None of the instruments disappear entirely, but some come to the fore while others recede into the background.

Just as working the faders is the best way to get across the artist's vision, turning up the volume on the elements of your story that showcase your accomplishments and lowering the volume on those that don't will give you the best shot at realizing yours. In some instances, however, the underlying track may still need some additional work first.

In the modern Christmas classic *Elf*, Will Ferrell plays a man named Buddy who accidentally stowed away in Santa's toy bag when he was an infant. When the movie begins, he is living as an elf in Santa's workshop without any knowledge that he is actually a human. As a result of being a human, he is the slowest, most inept toymaker in the North Pole, which causes him unceasing anguish. He eventually becomes so distressed by his subpar elfishness that, upon discovering his human heritage, he makes his way to New York City to find his birth father.

As he makes his way around New York City, he takes part in an epic snowball fight, designs a blockbuster department store display, and builds toys out of disassembled furniture. His proficiency at each of these tasks astounds everyone he encounters, none of whom understand how he is able to do what he does. What they don't realize is that the only difference between Buddy and themselves is that they weren't raised by elves at the North Pole.

Follow Buddy's example. Pinpoint a social or professional circle where you want to make a splash. Then identify a skill of yours that you take for granted. For example, maybe you're really good at making people feel comfortable socially. That's a natural talent that wouldn't attract much notice in a circle of party planners but that would come in handy if you were trying to crack a circle of tax accountants. Or perhaps you're awesome at fixing technical gizmos. Not a big deal in a circle of IT professionals, but if you need to get in good with a crowd of literary agents, becoming known as the resident tech whiz who is always willing to lend a hand could go a long way.

In short, figure out if your talent is in short supply among members of the new crowd you're looking to become part of, and if it doesn't cost you much to give a little of it away, do so, especially if it would appear particularly magical to those who don't possess it. Not only can leading with these sorts of abilities gain you entrée into circles that might otherwise be closed to you; it is often the first step in getting the people who matter most to the achievement of your goals to view you as miraculous.

UNEARTH THE GEM BURIED IN THE DIRT

While learning how to reframe the strengths we already have is one part of becoming a master hype artist, it is typically not enough. In fact, master hype artists mix in elements of precisely the opposite approach. When they manage to get the balance right, the result is pure magic.

Thomas Edison is known as the man who invented recorded sound, the light bulb, and motion pictures and in doing so single-handedly created the modern technological age. As usual, the story is far more complicated than the standard telling would have us believe. The reality is that Edison bumbled into his discovery of the principles that made the phonograph work while trying to improve the telegraph and then failed to recognize its importance for a decade. A number of people developed sources of electric light before he did, and even after his lab perfected the design of the light bulb, he couldn't figure out how to make it work on a large scale. As for the movie camera, he wasn't even in town when that was invented. One of his assistants conceived of it and built it while Edison was away trying to create a new kind of mining equipment.

When reporters of Edison's day dubbed him the "Wizard of Menlo Park," they were describing what they saw as the magic of his technological inventiveness. But Edison's real feat as a magician was that someone like him was able to become the foremost celebrity of his era.

Not only was Thomas Edison a far less accomplished inventor than his legend would suggest; he was also a thoroughly uncharismatic human being. He had a great deal of difficulty engaging in social pleasantries, which made relationships tough to build and maintain. When anyone dropped by to see him, including investors and business partners, he would find any reason he could to avoid emerging from his lab to spend time with them.

For many entrepreneurs, having the kind of personality that regularly alienated your most vital financial backers and professional connections would be a career-ending flaw. But Edison overcame this by reframing his greatest weakness as his most notable strength.

For example, when Edison's company was nothing more than a fledgling producer of small improvements to telegraph equipment, he worked with a publicity agent to spread a story about an associate who found him asleep at his desk at midnight to discover, upon his waking, that the inventor had gotten married earlier that day. The same publicist regularly "confided" to reporters about his employer's habit of working for days straight without stopping to eat or sleep. Later in his career, he installed a punch clock so that any members of the press who dropped by could see how long he had worked that week without stopping.

Before Edison, the dominant image of a "man of science" was that of a gentleman scholar like Charles Darwin, who spent a mere four hours a day working on his groundbreaking theory of natural selection. The archetype of the endlessly toiling genius in the lab was perhaps Edison's greatest invention. It was what allowed him to reframe his reclusiveness as a superhuman quality. It was what made him surprising and worthy in the eyes of the public—which, combined, turned him into a modern miracle that people couldn't get enough of.

Hype artists recognize what many of us do not—that what we see as extraordinary qualities are often inverted weaknesses. The magus finds the gem buried in the dirt of his greatest weakness and broadcasts it as such.

From an early age, Andy Warhol had plenty of artistic talent. But that was about all. He was scrawny, awkward, and effeminate in an age of World War II heroes and brawny leading men. He was shy to an almost pathological degree. He had a pallid complexion and a head of hair that had begun thinning when he was barely out of his teens.

But Warhol realized his weaknesses were good soil for growing his myth. He accentuated his small scrawny frame with the striped shirts, leather jackets, and tight-fitting pants that made him stand out in every crowd and would make him a fashion icon. He took advantage of his natural shyness to fashion a laconic communication style that would become legendary. Even his thinning hair and pallid complexion served as the canvas for his silver wig and otherworldly presence.

The approach that Edison and Warhol used requires a great deal of courage. The society we live in trains us from an early age to reject or correct what it collectively sees as flaws. When we do sense there's a certain aspect of our character that doesn't fit the commonly accepted mold of strength or competence, we typically respond by suppressing that part of ourselves. While this may help us fit in, it also causes us to lose whatever magic we might once have naturally possessed.

To regain your power, you need to begin by severing the mental connections between society's judgments and your inherent attributes. It's hard to do but worth it. If you only focus on promoting those parts of yourself that everyone else agrees are strengths, you severely limit your ability to stand out and transfix people with your uniqueness. Instead, go out of your way to face those parts of yourself that the general consensus says are not worthwhile or normal.

Do you have a certain trait you've long been self-conscious about? Do you have an eccentricity you've taken pains to hide? Pieces of yourself that other people think are weird or useless? Think back to your childhood. Can you remember being made fun of because of a certain aspect of your personality and then vowing not to act that way anymore? Were there places you went to in your daydreams that the world convinced you were unacceptable? List them all. Don't hold back.

Next, for each of these traits, think of a way to reframe it into a positive. Nestled into every one of the quirky elements that you have long suspected makes you a bit of a misfit is a golden nugget from which you can refashion yourself as a magus.

From all of these, choose the one that seems the most intriguing. The more sharply it stands out from the tenor of your time, the more likely it is that it contains the magic you are looking for. This is the foundation upon which you should begin building your persona. Once you've decided upon your magical power, weave it into every element of how you present yourself. Embody it whenever you communicate with the world—whether in a talk that could decide the course of your career or in a one-on-one conversation with a member of your extended social circle.

To make yourself appear miraculous, you must establish yourself as an unusually worthy character who never fails to generate surprises. If you're one of the few Richard Bransons of the world who has the stomach for death-defying transatlantic crossings and the like, by all means go for it. But if you're more like the rest of us, learn how to work your faders to emphasize your worthiest parts while at the same time surprising us by turning your so-called weaknesses inside out. More often than not, you'll find this is where the most attractive and magnetic parts of yourself reside.

Putting It into Practice

- Make one list of all your strengths and another of all your weaknesses. Put aside the weaknesses. Over the next week, you are going to practice not mentioning any of them.
- After a week, return to your list of weaknesses. Think about how you might flip each into a strength. Choose one of these newly discovered strengths and find ways to slip mentions of them into your various communications—whether one-on-one conversations or promotional materials.
- Develop your story. Come up with a ready-made narrative that explains how you got where you are. There are many storytelling structures out there to help you mold your tale (the hero's journey, the three-act structure, etc.). Fit *your* story into one of them to make it more compelling.

HYPE STRATEGY #7

FIND A VOID AND FILL IT

People are constantly giving out signals as to what they lack. They long for completeness, whether the illusion of it or the reality, and if it has to come from another person, that person has tremendous power over them.

—ROBERT GREENE

On the evening before April Fool's Day 1848, 14-year-old Maggie Fox and her 11-year-old sister Kate knocked at the door of their neighbor's home in the farm town of Hydesville, New York. The two girls seemed to be filled with both fear and excitement in equal measure. They told their neighbor they wanted her to see something that they had been experiencing with increasing regularity but that no one outside their household knew about. Curious, she followed them back to their house.

85

The girls' mother awaited them. Instead of greeting their neighbor, she stared blankly at a wall. Then, without warning she cried out.

"Now count five!"

The neighbor watched as the Fox sisters huddled together on their bed and focused trancelike on an indefinable point in the distance. After a stretch of silence, as if in response to some ineffable energy, a sound rang out.

Five disembodied knocks.

After she left, the incident was all the neighbor could think about. She told everyone she knew. Before long, people all over town were talking about it. Soon after that, people across the region were telling stories about the sisters, and not always in a positive light.

Eventually, the Fox sisters announced publicly that they would give a demonstration to prove the veracity of the claims. The resulting showcase took place at the largest performance hall in Rochester, New York, which was filled by 700 people. The sisters were thoroughly searched. They were bound and gagged as two acclaimed fraud busters looked on.

Nevertheless, to the astonishment of the assembled, the rapping noises rang out loud and clear. It was true! The Fox sisters could communicate with the dead.

The movement they birthed, *spiritualism*, would go on to become one of the biggest new phenomena of the nineteenth century, and it can be traced directly back to this moment.

Spiritualism was based on the belief that there are certain "mediums" who are tuned into the metaphysical realm. Not long after the Fox sisters' emergence, people—mainly women—all over the country were claiming to have this ability. Séances became regular occurrences (attended, again, mainly by women)—and, in many cases, big business for those who organized them.

It went on for decades. And then, after nearly a lifetime of promoting this new gospel, Maggie Fox decided she had had enough. She renounced all the claims she had ever made about her uncanny abilities. In front of an audience of 2,000 people at the New York Academy of Music, she showed how she was able to crack the joints in her toes and knuckles in a way that resonated loudly in the space around her while remaining completely motionless. It was this, rather than any spirits of the deceased, that had caused the rapping.

In the wake of her revelation, you might assume the hordes of disillusioned believers would have become complete skeptics, or would have at least retreated into traditional religion. Not so. Instead, a rash of new movements such as Christian Science, Theosophy, and New Age sprang up, with former spiritualists flooding their ranks.

During the mid-nineteenth century, rapid industrialization, new scientific discoveries, and technologies like the locomotive and telegraph were throwing long-held certainties into disarray. And when the Civil War broke out in the 1860s, an entire generation of sons and brothers was annihilated. Those affected most deeply by these alterations to the fabric of society had the least power. The grief of women regarding the upending of the only areas where they had any agency—religion and family—found its expression in spiritualism and its descendants.

By giving disoriented, grieving, disenfranchised women a vehicle for connecting with memories of their loved ones, the Fox sisters and their successors filled a major void for a neglected group whose members had few means of giving voice to their emptiness.

Contented people are not as easily influenced as the rest of us. Luckily for hype artists, no one stays content for very long.

While dissatisfaction is the default human condition, it tends to be difficult for people to accept that their dissatisfaction springs from circumstances outside their control. As such, we constantly (albeit subconsciously) look for mechanisms, systems, and answers, even when there are none.

Tim Ferriss is an author, entrepreneur, venture capitalist, podcaster, and lifestyle engineer. But his real talent is his ability to give the impression that he has the secret to filling a strain of mass emptiness that is specific to our current moment.

Ferriss observed the deep lack of fulfillment on the part of the millions of white-collar employees spending countless hours in cubicle farms. As soon as he zeroed in on this, he saw his opportunity. He preached that there was no reason to live this way. He said that you could automate your work and live a fulfilling, semiretired life for now and forever.

Jackpot!

If you compare the number of *The 4-Hour Workweek* readers who have achieved the kind of low-toil success Ferriss claims is possible with the number of those who sing his praises, you'll find a very small ratio. Yet that doesn't stop them from coming back for more.

When building your own hype strategy, follow Ferriss's example. Start by taking stock of the zeitgeist. Are there any changes—in technology, politics, or norms—that are making certain segments of the population feel left behind? Make it a point to find out which people feel the most affected.

When you pinpoint a void shared by multiple people, you gain the opportunity to exert incredible influence over them. Organic megamarket chain Whole Foods has made a fortune by giving baby boomers (and their children) a way to recapture the lost idealism of their youth through their purchasing power. Harley-Davidson reinvigorated its brand by appealing to Middle Americans who felt a lack of adventure in their lives. Calvin Klein launched the first mass market designer jeans by giving workaday people trapped in routine lives a taste of subversion, as hinted at by teenage model Brooke Shields who told them, "Nothing gets between me and my Calvins." It is a fail-safe formula for anyone looking to generate fanatical fans, followers, or customers.

BECOME AN ANCHOR IN THE RIPTIDES OF LIFE

How do I understand this dynamic so well? Because I too have fallen under its sway.

When I was a freshman at the University of Pennsylvania, I went from being a highly driven Ivy League–bound academic star of my high school class to a lost and lonely kind of guy. Early in the year, I realized what had kept me moving forward for so long was an obsession with getting into a top college. Now I had achieved my goal, and I couldn't figure out how to best take advantage of actually being there.

By Thanksgiving, my high school girlfriend had dumped me for another guy. In the midst of my heartbreak, I decided to refocus my attention on making my lifelong dream of becoming a writer happen. But when I told my father I planned to organize my coursework around this objective, he told me I was wasting my time. Within a week, he had sent me a printout of all the finance and accounting classes I should be taking.

Needless to say, I was feeling pretty blue when a friend of mine handed me *The Fountainhead* by Ayn Rand and told me it was exactly what I needed to read. It was—or at least, that was how it felt at the time. I tore through the 753-page book in a week and a half.

The tale of the uncompromising architect who would sooner blow up a construction site than compromise any of his designs struck me as revelatory. Here was a blueprint for how to live my life. I would pursue my art, no matter what anyone said. (Take that, dad!) And in the meantime, I would hit the gym four times a week while shoveling brown rice and protein powder down my throat to forge myself into the pillar of iron every real man should be.

Over the course of the ensuing 20 years, I have become increasingly less a fan of Ayn Rand's writing and her ideas, but my interest in her methods of persuasion has grown.

When I return to her books today, it's striking how little her characters resemble any human beings I have actually encountered. They never experience confusion or doubt or internal conflict of any kind. They are perfect machines of self-sufficiency and single-minded pursuit of their interests. Considering that Rand was up front about her desire to use her writing to spread the gospel of a philosophy she called "objectivism"—the idea that unregulated capitalism and unmitigated selfishness are the ultimate good—it is no surprise that the personal qualities of her characters line up completely with her worldview.

In her books, as well as in her nonfiction writings and her talks, Rand provides a ready-made set of solutions that her readers and followers could turn to whenever it was unclear what path they should follow. She even created a specialized vocabulary for her ideas, with terms like "second-handers," "subjectivists," and "psycho-epistemology," which followers could refer to and use to defend their new all-encompassing scheme for organizing reality.

Once you have identified a void, you must frame whatever you are selling as a comprehensive solution for filling it. There are many ways to make this happen. Devise a specialized vocabulary to represent the all-in-one solutions potential followers can apply to all that ails them. Create a manifesto or list of "rules for life" that tells people exactly what they must do to be successful, happy, or fully realized in a world where everything is rapidly changing.

Whatever specific tactics you land on, the important thing is that you speak about the new reality you are presenting without doubt, with total confidence, and in black-and-white terms. Give people a steady anchor in an out-of-control world, and they will be yours.

BECOMING A MASTER OF PROPHECY

There is another reliable strategy for gaining influence by filling a void. It is a method that master hype artists have been using since before the age of the ancient magi and continues to exert a powerful pull well into the twenty-first century.

I still remember when I first heard the name "Nate Silver." It was during the election of 2008, and I was in a bad way once again. I was extremely unhappy in my job, a vice president of Solution Development (whatever that means) at a company that operated call centers in rural Appalachia. I couldn't shake the sense that everything I had ever wanted to do with my life was slipping right past me and it was my own fault.

After engaging in a tremendous amount of self-abuse, I finally gathered up the guts to quit. That would have been great, except the economy collapsed. And this was no ordinary economic downturn. It was the Great Recession. Friends were losing their jobs all around me. It looked like a depression was right around the corner.

Yet another void had appeared in my soul.

But then, as I saw it at the time, a champion emerged into the dark morass of the first decade of the twenty-first century. Barack Obama. Like so many other ex-hipster, still-somewhat-young urban professionals, I must admit I became a little obsessed with the presidential candidate. The line between my future happiness and the outcome of the election became somewhat indistinguishable to me. However, other than casting my single vote six months down the road, there was nothing I could do to affect the election.

Until FiveThirtyEight entered my life, that is.

Nate Silver was a statistician who had already made a bit of a name for himself using data analysis to help professional baseball teams draft players. Now he had entered the realm of politics. On his blog, Silver followed the election from, as he presented it, a purely statistical point of view. As he gathered data from polls, demographic assessments, electors, and various other sources I still don't quite understand, he would make forecasts about whether John McCain or Barack Obama would win the electoral votes of each of the various states.

What made Silver's approach so refreshing and addictive was that it was apparently based on concreteness. While the pundits shouted their opinions and spoke from their emotions, Silver repeatedly stated that his personal political views had no bearing whatsoever on his forecasts. They were based on mathematics. They were based on the rules of nature. As a person who felt like he had little control over his own life, having someone tell me there was a set of laws, patterns, and equations that could indicate what was going to happen was incredibly comforting.

In reality, though, my power didn't change at all. I still only had one vote. What Nate Silver did was make me *feel* like I had more control over the outcome. In return for this feeling, I paid him with attention to his blog and dollars for his book.

Prophecy is an incredibly effective sales tactic.

While there were quite a few people who felt like I did about Silver before the election, it was when he correctly predicted its outcome that his star truly soared. His book *The Signal and the Noise* quickly shot up every bestseller list. His blog became more popular than ever. He appeared as a guest on every political talk show. ESPN hired him to create a website that would make forecasts about every conceivable element of the world through data analysis.

One of the hardest truths to face as we grow up is that what lies before us is an infinite blind spot. There is no way to know what the future holds because, by definition, it hasn't happened yet. It's terrifying. So is the idea that whatever adversity we are currently facing might never get better.

There have always been prophets, oracles, and soothsayers. In our scientifically minded society, they simply go by different names.

Consider the financial newsletters for which experts charge large sums of money to lay out a web of signs of what stocks to buy and indicators of which companies will supposedly go up or down in value. Consider the futurists to whom Fortune 100 companies pay hundreds of thousands of dollars per engagement to predict social, technological, and economic trends. Consider the scads of market research firms, which use data and statistics to show clients what *their* clients will be buying in a few years hence.

Masters of hype play with this intense human desire to control the uncontrollable. They understand that people want to believe there is a code to the unknowable. By positioning yourself as one of the select few that can interpret this code, you become indispensable.

So how can you capture some of the magic of prophecy in your own career? Is it simply a matter of mastering the right statistical formulas? Patterns? Entrails? Tea leaves? Star charts?

Don't worry. It's much simpler than that. To become a prophet, start making prophecies.

First, get into the habit of watching trends. Imagine these trends stretched out into the future and picture how they might unfold and evolve. Armed with these observations, you can start making predictions. Make a lot of them, but do it quietly, informally, and on a small scale. Remember, you are still conducting tests of your ideas. Most of the predictions you make at this early stage will be wrong. As such, you'll want your numerous bad calls to fade away and be forgotten.

Even if you do miss the mark, a self-styled prophet can always recover. When his "scientific" system failed spectacularly to predict the defeat of Hillary Clinton in 2016, Nate Silver's confidence never wavered. When one reporter asked him what had happened, the "Stats Wizard" looked at him and replied, "The models are right. It's the voters who are wrong."

His stance paid off. In 2018, both Georgetown University and Kenyon College honored him with the prestigious Doctor of Humane Letters degree. As for his fans, they are as devoted to him as they ever were.

But when one of your quiet predictions does turn out to be right, that's when it is time to ramp up both the volume and the boldness. Go public. Share what you prophesied far and wide. Create the impression that you knew what was coming all along. This is what most people want. The majority of us know, deep down, that no one can actually predict the future. What we crave is the feeling that there is someone more knowledgeable than we are who can show us where to cast our lots.

Making prophecies is just another method for giving people a solid foundation in the face of uncertainty. The more ways you find to do this, the more your power to influence outcomes in your own life and career will grow.

Putting It into Practice

- Take stock of changes in the world that are especially disorienting. Research which groups of people feel the most affected by them. If whatever you're selling addresses any of these changes, you've found your target market.
- Whether you're writing articles, speaking, giving interviews, etc., tell people exactly what they must do to be successful, happy, or fully realized. Whatever specific tactics you land on, the important thing is that you speak about the new reality with complete confidence as the *only* solution to their problems.
- Make lots of predictions—quietly, informally, and on a small scale. When one of your forecasts pans out, trumpet your success on a wide scale. Don't forget to say "I told you so."

HYPE STRATEGY #8

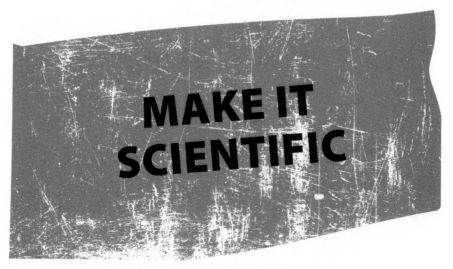

MAKE IT SCIENTIFIC

Consultants, if they are wise, limit their claims of expertise to just those subjects in which no one else can claim to know what they are doing.
—MATTHEW STEWART

Martin Seligman, professor of psychology at the University of Pennsylvania, launched his career by administering painful electric shocks to dogs to determine what causes mammals to succumb to despair. He coined the term "learned helplessness," wrote a book about it, and got hired by the CIA to help put together its "enhanced interrogation" program. Then he got himself elected president of the American Psychological Association (APA).

Always a man with a sense of the well-timed career move, he used his new role at the APA to shift focus. At his inauguration, he announced that psychology had, for far too long, concentrated on mental illness and the negative side of the human experience. It was time, he proclaimed, to build a new "positive psychology," which would instead be about making healthy people happier.

Since then, the popularity of the professor's work has exploded. He regularly receives invitations to give keynote addresses at some of the world's largest corporations. He had a personal audience with the prime minister of Great Britain. He has provided coaching to hundreds of people at a time on conference calls costing $2,000 a pop.

Martin Seligman was certainly not the first person to promote the benefits of positive thinking. Before him, though, the concept tended to repel as many people as it attracted, carrying with it a faint whiff of the tent revival. Seligman changed this. He brought positive thinking into the laboratory and the boardroom.

Unlike his predecessors, Seligman regularly refers to statistics and equations and uses high-flown terminology. His words serve as the equivalent of a doctor's white coat. They seem authoritative, so we don't question them.

While Seligman's ideas have been widely embraced, a few brave souls have stepped forward to challenge him. In particular, the journalist Barbara Ehrenreich, in her book *Bright-Sided: How Positive Thinking Is Undermining America*, dug into some of positive psychology's most deeply held tenets.

At one point, Ehrenreich writes about how, during an interview with Seligman, she brought up discrepancies she had uncovered in some of the mathematical formulas he claims proves the effectiveness of his concepts. Instead of presenting a logical rebuttal, the professor responded with a irritated comment about her lack of sophistication—perhaps a function of how rarely he is challenged.

During a lecture on positive psychology at the University of East London, a mathematician named Nick Brown listened to an acolyte of Seligman speak with reverence about the number 2.9013. According to the presenter, if the ratio of a person's total positive emotions to their negative emotions came out to 2.9013, the person had a flourishing life. Everyone in attendance seemed to accept this finding without question. Everything Brown knew about mathematics told him it was absurd.

"The idea that any aspect of human behavior or experience," Brown explained, "should be universally and reproducibly constant to five significant digits would, if proven, constitute a unique moment in the history of the social sciences."

Nick Brown published his insights in an academic paper. Hardly anyone paid attention.

What is it about Seligman's ideas that make them so attractive even when they fail to hold up under scrutiny?

Martin Seligman's math may be questionable, but his marketing is sound. He understands that while many Ivy League academics, corporate executives, and other power brokers tend to resist the fluffy positive thinking concepts used by the likes of preachers and New Age gurus, they cannot resist the persuasive appeal of these same ideas when packaged in hard science and big data.

It is a lesson you would do well to follow.

THE SCIENCE OF HYPE

In a series of experiments, psychologists Carl Hovland and Walter Weiss presented subjects with a series of arguments advocating for positions they disagreed with. In some instances, the new arguments were conveyed informally by people dressed in street clothes. In other cases, they were presented by people displaying obvious credentials.

The subjects who received the contrarian opinions from the more visibly credible figures changed their minds far more often than the first group, even though none of the so-called experts presenting their arguments ever offered any real proof of their expertise.

Why do otherwise intelligent people so readily trust these displays of credibility, regardless of whether that credibility is backed up in any meaningful way?

We simply cannot help it. It is how our brains are wired.

Popular science writer Leonard Mlodinow explored this concept in depth in his bestselling book *Subliminal: How Your Unconscious Mind Rules Your Behavior.* "We don't have the time or the mental bandwidth," he explains, "to observe and consider each detail of every item in our environment. Instead we employ a few salient traits that we do observe to assign the object to a category rather than the object itself."

In other words, our brains don't really care about digging into all the details that go into making someone a credible expert. What our mental circuitry does crave is shortcuts indicating the person we are thinking about following is smart and capable.

How can you benefit from this effect in your own career? For those on a traditional path, it is relatively simple. Enroll in the right educational programs; take the right tests; get the right degrees. However, it becomes more challenging for any of us whose trajectory is less well defined. If your goal, project, or concept is unusual, new, or original, the credibility signals people rely on to decide whether to trust you may not even exist yet.

That's when the tools, tactics, and strategies of the hype artist become incredibly valuable.

THE LONG LIFE OF SCIENTIFIC PRESENTATION

There are few accolades more prestigious in higher education than a master of business administration from Harvard Business School. Its alumni have filled the C-suites and corporate boards of America for more than a century. As the first postgraduate business school, HBS is the template for every MBA program that followed.

The principles on which the Harvard Business School curriculum is based come directly from the ideas of turn-of-the-twentieth century thinker and writer Frederick Winslow Taylor—the originator of a discipline called "scientific management."

In a series of lectures delivered from the study of his mansion in Chestnut Hill, Pennsylvania (later captured in his book *The Principles of Scientific Management*), Taylor told his devoted listeners the story of a machine shop that had hired him to advise the shop during the early days of his career. While there, he hit upon a method of using mathematical analysis and behavioral engineering to dramatically improve the efficiency of the company's pig iron loading operation.

His findings would go on to form the basis of a revolution in industrial organization. Moreover, the idea that you could manipulate the messy province of human behavior through precise measurement and strict control was irresistible to those tasked with educating future captains of industry.

Taylor explained increases in productivity with formulas such as $B = (p + [a + b + d + f + \text{distance hauled}/100 \times (c + e)]27/L)(1 + P)^*$. He presented instructions for how managers should interact with their workers in terms of unalterable principles having more in common with Newton's laws of thermodynamics than with the gut-based decision-making that had preceded him. He kept his rules and stories exactly the same from meeting to meeting and lecture to lecture.

To this day, much of what is taught about industrial production is based on what Frederick Taylor put forth. However, almost all of the broad, scientific principles he presented as ironclad facts were based on nothing more than a single, nonreproducible example.

Even the quickest deep dive into Taylor's "scientific management" would have revealed inconsistencies betraying a complete lack of true scientific method to anyone who might have cared to ask. Yet for the longest time, no one ever really did. Why? Because he unfailingly used a brand of scientific hype consisting of two equally balanced parts—data and certainty.

In the words of Matthew Stewart, who relates this story in his book *The Management Myth*, "Frederick Winslow Taylor told the pig-iron story so often and so well that . . . critics and sympathizers alike simply assumed it was true. But it was not."

The real world—especially when it comes to human behavior— is messy, and this is uncomfortable for many people. Formulas, laws, and unchanging principles allow people to feel they have a bulwark against this chaos, and they will pay a lot for this feeling.

Frederick Taylor's success didn't come about *because* his ideas were unsubstantiated but, rather, in spite of it. If you are struggling to gain traction around a legitimate new idea, business, or cause, elements of his strategy will prove useful in your mission to stand out and build momentum.

Always speak with complete certainty. Present your ideas as if they were truths on par with the theory of relativity. Use numbers. Find relevant statistics and cite them publicly whenever possible. Today, the internet allows you to access and compile real data from the widest variety of sources. Surround your claims with well-researched credibility signals, and you'll be able to create the Frederick Taylor effect on behalf of something real.

WHY ASK WHY?

In many ways, the digital age equivalent to Frederick Taylor's Chestnut Hill lectures are TED Talks (with the latter, of course, having a wider scope of distribution). It was as a result of a blockbuster TED Talk called "Start with Why" that Simon Sinek launched his career as a business guru. He subsequently published a book with the same title, which quickly became a bestseller. Then he parlayed that into a run of high-traffic YouTube videos and even higher-priced keynote speeches. With his serious air, professorial spectacles, and $10 words, Sinek comes across as the kind of guy who spends his days conducting lab research and writing academic papers.

Not so.

Before he became a professional guru, Simon Sinek worked in advertising. His tenure at Ogilvy & Mather and Euro RSCG taught him well how to sell his ideas in the form of books, talks, and consulting engagements.

According to Sinek, companies achieve enduring success by tapping into the human *neocortex*. Likewise, the reason passion is so important in business is because of the *limbic system*. Furthermore, our dependence on social media is all about *dopamine*.

Is all this accurate? I would argue it doesn't actually matter. Like Frederick Taylor, Sinek understands scientific packaging is one of the most effective sales strategies around. What makes his approach especially sophisticated is his use of a preexisting scientific vocabulary to add glitter to what might otherwise be common sense (and hence humdrum) concepts. In this regard, he comes from a proud tradition.

For instance, the word "halitosis" was almost completely unknown to the general public until the early twentieth century when a business owner named Gerard Lambert started using it to sell a new product called Listerine. By giving a mundane fact of life (bad breath) a scientific-sounding label, Lambert elevated the authority and desirability of his product many times over.

Sinek and Lambert have a lot in common. Repackaging kitchen table advice and popular wisdom in a gauze of neurons, dendrites, and hormones has helped the motivational speaker-slash-consultant create a movement.

Follow his example. Straight talk only goes so far. Sometimes it pays to overcomplicate simple messages. Make a list of $10 words, scientific terms, and obscure niblets of terminology and find ways to use them. Your reputation and authority will soar.

Another tactic Simon Sinek uses to get people to pay big money for his ideas is to position himself as the guy in charge without being too obvious about it. He is careful to speak in an unthreatening tone while at the same time choosing words that establish him as an undisputed alpha thinker.

Consider his most famous statement: "Start with why." He isn't making a suggestion about what you *might* want to try to do. He isn't presenting a possibility for you to consider. He is telling you what you *must* do if you want to achieve success. "Start with why" is a command. And people follow commands . . . when they come from a "trusted expert," that is.

Find ways to do the same in your business. Take your most important concepts and create a list of 10 punchy statements, each beginning with an action verb. When you tell people exactly what they should do, they will. And usually they won't even think about it first. Plus, the air of scientific authority in one area has a tendency to bleed into others.

In 2017 a Simon Sinek video began circulating on the internet about why millennials are such disappointments in the workplace.

In his telling, they were failed by their parents who "told them they were special all the time" and gave them "participation medals for coming in last."

Over the course of this monologue, Sinek proclaims that the science supporting this truth is "very clear" (of course) before going on to lay out the full scope of all the other psychological, sociological, and neurological reasons for this generation's shortcomings. Judging from its millions of views and enthusiastic comments, a good portion of the YouTube ecosystem considers this video to be on par with the collected works of Stephen Hawking in its ability to explain how the universe works.

But really, what percentage of millennials actually received participation trophies on a regular basis? Did millennials who grew up in Appalachia receive the same kind of parenting as those who grew up in Orange County? What about all the other generations who were called shiftless by their elders (see: lazy hippies and Generation X slackers)?

It is interesting how many people immediately accepted Sinek's explanation without questioning it. This is a testament to how well he understands how to deliver a message to ensure maximum buy-in. Sinek rarely casts his ideas as mere opinions. You will hardly ever hear him give the other side of the story or cite a scientific finding that doesn't support his argument. Not only does he proclaim ideas with utter confidence; he conveys them as immutable laws of nature.

Do like Sinek. If you're a reasonable human being, there's a good chance you have some doubts about some of your ideas. Keep your doubts to yourself. If you want to build a dedicated following, talk about your offer as if it is the one and only answer to the problems your clients and customers face. Combined with a healthy dose of so-called science and verbal jujitsu, this tactic will ensure your business grows like crazy—even if you didn't start with why.

BEYOND SCIENCE

According to the *Merriam-Webster* dictionary, the definition of the word "arbitrage" is "the nearly simultaneous purchase and sale of securities of foreign exchange in different markets in order to profit from price discrepancies." In other words, an equity trader might use the strategy of arbitrage by uncovering and buying an undervalued currency or commodity in their own national market and then selling it at a high price in a different national market where its perceived value is much higher.

In many ways, the concepts we have been discussing in this chapter are a kind of psychological arbitrage. They convey credibility in one area by importing less understood words, terms, and concepts from another. Science is one tool for achieving this effect. But there are others.

Qingchi "C Bin" Bin and Zeyu Zheng met as freshmen at Boston University in the winter of 2016. Both of them had moved to the United States from China in early adolescence, both struggled to adapt at first, and both eventually figured out how to crack their adopted country's social codes.

They became fast friends, with a bond forged from their common background and shared interest in entrepreneurship. They spent many late nights in their dorm rooms dreaming about new businesses they could start together.

During this period, the friends regularly spent time on Chinese social media platforms like Dedao, which most of their American classmates had never heard of. For a while, Bin and

Zheng used the platforms to stay on top of what was happening back home and to keep in touch with old friends. Soon, however, they began to notice an interesting trend. More and more users were attempting to promote themselves—their hobbies, interests, and small businesses—in an outgoing style that was practically nonexistent in the China they had left only a few years earlier. And they were doing so poorly.

Bin and Zheng soon realized that in the face of exponential economic growth, people in China were finally coming to terms with the need to engage in overt marketing and self-promotion.

Because both of them had had to learn to promote themselves socially in a way that didn't come naturally to either of them, it occurred to them they could deliver this knowledge to the Chinese market. But unlike an American who might try to teach self-promotion in China, they had an intimate understanding of what it would take to translate what they knew. They also had a unique cachet that came from straddling both worlds.

The friends cofounded a digital education company called VStarOne and quickly began making real money. They spent some of the money on themselves. They reinvested some of it into the business. Sometimes they did both at the same time.

For example, Zheng bought a Corvette. Now a Corvette is certainly a nice car, but it is nowhere near as costly or prestigious as a Lamborghini or Ferrari. But it *is* a car that is barely known in China. So when Zheng posted photos of himself next to it on Dedao, it appeared he owned a car even more exotic—and hence more rare and prestigious—than top European models.

As the pair's fortunes and client base grew further, they realized they needed a team to help them out, but they didn't want the overhead of permanent office space and payroll. So they built a remote team, began to work out of various luxury hotels (a credibility signifier), and posted photos of themselves operating in the "workplace of the future." This increased their prestige even further.

How do I know so much about these guys? About a year and a half ago they contacted me about getting some coverage in *Forbes*, where I was writing a column at the time. I liked their story, and I thought they had a good product, so I agreed to cover them. They proceeded to spread the word about the article like crazy to their Chinese audience. Because *Forbes* is an American publication, it holds a level of prestige even beyond what it carries here. They used it to raise their audience's perceptions of them. Their customer base and revenue immediately experienced another spike.

Arbitrage.

Throughout this chapter we have discussed hype artists who have used scientific lingo to get people to accept what they offered without question. We have also examined entrepreneurs who have found credibility in uncommon places and used it to persuade people to give them a chance. In a digitally enhanced world where blatantly false claims can be uncovered in no time, pure deceit will only subvert your goals. Fortunately, even the most upright businesspeople and creators can use the underlying principles we've discussed at every stage of their careers. Dig deep and find exalted words for everyday things. Look for arbitrage opportunities in areas in which you can see details that members of your potential audience cannot. And always remember that credibility is in the eye of the beholder. It is up to you to shape how you are beheld.

Putting It into Practice

- Instead of using jargon that other people have come up with, create your own. Use it whenever possible. Doing this will convey instant expertise.
- Take your most important concepts and develop 10 punchy statements that each start with an action verb.
- Use numbers. Research statistics and cite them publicly. Refer to mathematical formulas. Talk about data. Even just using the word "data" will provide much of the desired effect.

PRAYERS, SPELLS, AND SYMBOLS

Frequency of language use and imagery matters.
The more frequent the language use or imagery,
the more strengthening occurs.

—GEORGE LAKOFF

Human beings like to think we make decisions based on things that matter. If we take on a project, it's because we genuinely feel it's a great opportunity. If we buy a pricey product, it's because its benefits outweigh its costs. And if we spend time and money on entertainment, it's because we have good taste.

In truth, the forces that influence us—that draw us in and get us excited—typically have less to do with the content of the message than with how it is delivered.

From Julius Caesar's "Veni, vidi, vici" to Patrick Henry's "Give me liberty or give me death," the most skilled political outsiders have always used sloganeering, radical simplification, and relentless repetition to help them gain and consolidate power. When the leaders of the French Revolution decided they needed to transform what was then an unruly mob into a revolutionary army, they simply supplied the rallying cry, "Liberté, égalité, fraternité," and when the Bolsheviks wanted to mobilize a peasant army, they led the peasants in the singing of "L'Internationale." These political hype artists all intuitively grasped the principle that simple, gut-level language works far better than complex intellectual arguments.

In recent years, a number of neuroscientists, psychologists, and linguists have been getting to the bottom of why we so readily respond to some patterns of sounds and images more than others. In three separate studies, University of Michigan psychologist Robert Zajonc showed subjects a random selection of nonsense words, Chinese characters, and photos of strangers. He repeated each word or image up to 25 times. Zajonc uncovered a direct correlation between the amount of exposure to a word or image and the subject's perception of its favorability.

Using fMRI imaging, neuroscientists have more recently demonstrated that the brain's hippocampus relies on repetition to imprint information. Since we human beings are nature's foremost learning machines, it is no surprise repetition exerts such a hold on us.

The Rhode Island School of Design, or RISD, is perhaps the premier college of visual and practical arts in the United States. Its graduates regularly emerge as pioneers in painting, sculpture, photography, architecture, industrial design, and textiles science.

The facilities are first rate, the curriculum is demanding, and students take their work very seriously. It was at RISD that Rebecca Allen developed the basic tenets of computer art. It was where Dale Chihuly began to revolutionize the art of glass installation sculpture.

So when the pasty kid with the ratty T-shirts was spending all his time there in the basement printing the same goofy sticker over and over, it was no surprise a number of people complained he was wasting important resources on a bunch of nonsense.

Born in 1967, Shepard Fairey had grown up in a world where branding was as much a part of the firmament as earth, fire, water, and air. Jingles on the radio. Billboards on the way to school. TV commercials when you got home. Ads splashed across the sides of buses and park benches. Fairey, on the other hand, saw himself as a nonconformist. He liked art. He liked skateboarding. He liked punk rock. He liked giving the finger to the mind-numbing indoctrination the mainstream world accepted so easily.

In Fairey's view, the brands and slogans of corporate America were not much different from Soviet propaganda. To prove his point, he decided to conduct an experiment.

"I was teaching a friend how to make stencils in the summer of 1989," explains Fairey, "and I looked for a picture to use in the newspaper, and there just happened to be an ad for wrestling with Andre the Giant, and I told him that he should make a stencil of it. He said 'Nah, I'm not making a stencil of that, that's stupid!' but I thought it was funny, so I made the stencil and I made a few stickers."

Fairey made his image as simple and stylized as a hammer and sickle or fast-food logo—monochrome and stripped of all detail. Then he taxed the capabilities of his school's silk screen machine to reproduce the image ad nauseam. After he had enough of them to fill the better part of his dorm room, the real work began. Each night, when other students were sleeping or partying, he snuck around and pasted the stickers on every street sign, lamppost, and municipal fuse box he could find.

If the goal of the artist's experiment was to demonstrate the power of mindless repetition, regardless of the subject matter, it succeeded to an extraordinary degree. Stickers and stencils soon bloomed all over Providence, as followers and imitators picked up where he left off. Before long, you couldn't go to any major metropolitan area in the United States without seeing Andre the Giant.

Viewed rationally, a flag, coat of arms, corporate logo, or official seal has no more inherent meaning than a decal of a professional wrestler. However, repeated enough times in a simple enough form, any symbol—or catchphrase or slogan—acquires emotional resonance and memorability.

As a hype artist, you need to use this feature of the human brain to your benefit. Stop overcomplicating and overexplaining your products, services, messages, or causes. Instead, boil down your central idea into a pithy, memorable phrase or image and repeat it in as many forms and through as many media as you can get access to. When people can't escape your rallying cry or symbol or standard, they will come to adopt it as their own even if they initially rejected or ignored it.

At the same time, repeating yourself is not sufficient for binding adoring hordes to you, your cause, or your products. Not all phrases and images are created equal. To truly worm your way into the hearts and minds of your audience, there is an intricate tapestry of language and form you must master.

AS MALLEABLE AS A BABY'S NOGGIN

In his book *The Language Instinct,* Dr. Steven Pinker, director of Cognitive Neuroscience at MIT, explores why we so often respond more viscerally to the form of a message than to its actual content. "Humans like anything that purifies the basics of their world," he writes, "and that resonates with the way the brain decodes the blooming, buzzing confusion out there. We like stripes and plaids, we like periodic and harmonic sounds, and we like rhymes."

Laura Ries has built her career around this concept.

Ries first made a name for herself at the New York agency TBWA, running major accounts like Woolite and Evian. Eventually she went into business with her father, a man who knew a thing or two about marketing in his own right. Al Ries was the person who, along with coauthor Jack Trout, first described a new concept called brand "positioning" in a series of articles in *Advertising Age.* A book based on the concept went on to sell 1.5 million copies and became part of the curriculum of almost as many Marketing 101 courses.

Laura Ries went on to carve out her own area of expertise by reverse-engineering what makes certain brand slogans explode while others flop. And as she tells it, the brain's default vocabulary is made up of images.

"Specific names that conjure up mental images are more powerful than abstract names," says Ries. "In the academic world, what do researchers call a 50-page document they might have spent months or years working on? A paper. . . . What does a business executive call an appointment to serve on the board of directors of a Fortune 500 company? A seat. Burger King is a better name for a food chain than Sandwich King. Red Lobster is a better name for a seafood chain than Red Seafood."

Ries was certainly not the first person to remark on the benefits of using slogans that evoke imagery. But her unique contribution has been to figure out the more subtle elements that determine which ones actually stick.

As Ries notes, human beings have been using hooks like rhyme and alliteration to imprint their ideas into people's brains for as long as anyone can remember. It is these hooks, when combined with imagery and relentless repetition, that really move the minds, mouths, and feet of millions. Once you become aware of Laura Ries's philosophy of sloganeering, you start to see it everywhere.

BMW was only the eleventh bestselling European car import until it rolled out its slogan "The ultimate driving machine," a phrase that evoked an actual entity of steel and rubber zipping down an actual road. In less than three years, it was the most popular luxury vehicle brand in the world. But when it later abandoned that slogan in favor of the vague replacement "Joy," Mercedes quickly overtook it again.

American public opinion was strongly tilted against entry into World War I. President Woodrow Wilson tasked the Creel Committee to fix this, which it did by means of the alliterative slogan "The *war* to end all *wars*." By 1917, 1.5 million young men had volunteered for the strong possibility of dying in a trench.

And then there was Aimee Semple McPherson.

McPherson emerged from her era's mess of tent show preachers, holy rollers, and self-styled prophets to become the first modern evangelist superstar. Her Angelus Temple became the first megachurch in the 1920s, and her International Institute of Four Square Evangelism brought in $1.5 million a year ($18 million in present-day money).

One of McPherson's favorite sermons kicked off with the preacher thundering into her church, straddling a motorcycle, dressed as a traffic cop. When she reached the front, she would spin her bike into a halt, blow her whistle, and shout: "Stop! You're speeding to hell!"

In another sermon, she described civilization as a carousel that periodically wore out, needing a master mechanic (such as Jesus . . . or Sister Aimee) to come along and fix it. Her title for this sermon? "The Merry Go Round Broke Down."

And then there was one of her best-known productions, in which members of her congregation would march throughout the church depicting figures like St. Paul, Joan of Arc, and Nero. McPherson's name for this theatrical display? "The March of the Martyrs."

Rhyme. Alliteration. Concrete action. And plenty of imagery. Sister Aimee may have loved her flock, but there was no way she was going to rely on mere explanations of God's Kingdom to get her followers to pin their banknotes to the clothing lines she regularly strung from one end of her church to the other.

In describing the sway leaders like McPherson hold over their followers, Gustave Le Bon writes, "Whatever be the ideas suggested to crowds, they can only exercise influence on condition that they assume a very absolute, uncompromising, and simple shape."

Timothy Leary began his career as a fairly conventional scholar and scientist. After completing his PhD in clinical psychology, he served as director of psychiatric research at the Kaiser Family Foundation and lectured at Harvard University. But by 1966, Leary had become notorious in certain elite circles for his contrarian ideas and lifestyle experiments.

A few years earlier, he had first encountered lysergic acid diethylamide—or LSD. Eventually the potential of this compound to alter perception became the dominant strand in his work and then his life. He left his post as a Harvard psychology professor and began to consider what to do with his newfound knowledge about the true nature of reality. It became increasingly clear to him that he could not keep these insights to himself. What he now knew could remake society, and it was his duty to spread it to the masses. Yet Leary knew his impact was still limited.

He needed to do something different.

The answer came during a lunch with Marshall McLuhan, an already famous professor of media and communications. After listening to his friend's problem, McLuhan told him he was going about it all the wrong way. If he really wanted to attract a mass audience, he would have to model those who had already been doing it successfully for the better part of a century. The masterminds of Madison Avenue.

This advice was hard for Leary to accept. His mission, as he saw it, was about taking down precisely the kind of empty commercialism the advertising industry specialized in promoting. He agonized over the decision nonstop.

But ultimately Leary went along with his friend's opinion. He spent weeks poring over jingles, slogans, and ad copy. He racked his brain, trying to figure out how to summarize the profundity of his realization with the kind of pithy phrase that was typically used to sell hamburgers and lawnmowers.

And then it hit him:

Turn on, tune in, drop out.

The slogan had it all. It was alliterative and punchy. It was active. It was visual.

In early 1967, Leary was invited to give a speech at the first Human Be-In in San Francisco's Golden Gate Park. The attendees were young and shaggy—a mix of hippies, bikers, and runaways. But the savvy former professor had the good sense to match his speech with the tenor of his audience. To say the speech was short on specifics would be an understatement. In fact, most of it consisted of a single, rhythmic, alliterative phrase repeated over and over and over:

> *Turn on, tune in, drop out.*
> *Turn on, tune in, drop out.*
> *Turn on, tune in, drop out.*

It had the desired effect. From that point forward, the rate at which Leary's message spread was nothing short of remarkable. Drawing directly from the establishment's bag of tricks, Timothy Leary created the rallying cry the counterculture would come together around in their attempt to change the world.

What makes "Turn on, tune in, drop out" especially effective is that it works on multiple levels. It certainly has all the hypnotic hallmarks of repetition, alliteration, and rhythm our brains readily respond to. At the same time, it provides marching orders to its audience.

As we've seen many times throughout this book, people—especially people in groups—follow those who give them a blueprint for how to feel and act, as long as they don't believe that is what's happening. When you are developing a slogan that describes what you offer, make it concrete. But when you are developing a slogan designed to give people guidance on how to act, keep it vague.

What were people turning onto, tuning into, or dropping out of? How exactly are people making America great again? Who knows? It's better that way. Let the members of your audience fill in their own meanings. This way, they will inevitably attribute any positive changes they make to you but won't be able to hold you responsible for any missteps.

THE CREATIVE POWER OF REPETITION, RHYTHM, AND RHYME

Sometime in the early fifties, Todd Storz and Bill Stewart went to Omaha to turn around the city's last-place radio station KOWH. There were already five other stations in town that featured a varied mix of live performances, drama, and news. They tried anything they thought might get people's attention and keep them tuned in. Different blends of material. Different on-air personalities. Different promotions. But they quickly discovered that in this heartland city, no one was exactly clamoring for new forms of cultural expression.

After months of futile effort, they fell back on an approach many great men before them had resorted to when faced with seemingly insurmountable obstacles.

They went out to get drunk.

The two executives ordered beers, found stools with a good view of the room, and settled in to watch the small crowd. Actually, Storz and Stewart had a secondary motivation for visiting the local tavern. The bar had a jukebox, and they wanted to get a firsthand feel for the tastes of their market. What they quickly confirmed was that these tastes were about as bland as Omaha's featureless terrain.

Although the jukebox had 60-plus selections on offer, patrons kept picking the same song—a trite and banal ditty called "The Music Goes Round and Round." Someone would pop a coin into the slot, and the tune would play. It would end, and then a minute or two later someone else would do the same thing. And so on.

It would have been one thing if their fellow drinkers had been dancing or even humming along. But their reaction was nil—the song more or less served as background music for patrons talking about their work and their worries and their lives. Yet they kept playing it.

As it often did, Todd Storz's mind eventually drifted back to the war. This night he thought back to when he and his buddies would go out for R&R and that, come to think about it, they didn't act all too differently from the working folks here in the Midwest. Whenever the soldiers managed to find a jukebox, they too would play the same songs over and over. Far from home, they just wanted something familiar.

In that moment, something clicked for Storz. He looked up from his beer and immediately shared his insight with his partner. Life is full of uncertainty and unasked-for change. Maybe they— and their competitors—had it wrong. Maybe people didn't want variety after all. Maybe KOWH could solve its problem by selling repetition itself.

It was the breakthrough they had been looking for. Back at the station, they immediately put their new idea into practice. They studied charts of top-selling records in trade publications like *Billboard*. They built tight playlists that mirrored these charts. They commanded and cajoled skeptical disc jockeys into not playing anything else.

Within months, KOWH went from having less than 5 percent of market share to regularly attracting nearly half of all radio listeners in the city.

The new format quickly spread beyond Omaha—first to other cities in the Midwest, then outward to the coasts. By the mid-fifties, repetitive hit-based programming was the standard for most radio stations across America. Soon the new format had a name: *Top 40 radio.*

Storz and Stewart were thrilled by the profits their innovation commanded. As Todd Storz explained years later: "I do not believe there is such thing as better or inferior music. If the public suddenly showed a preference for Chinese music, we would play it."

But not everyone was pleased by their breakthrough. Old stalwarts of the music biz lambasted what they saw as a crass appeal to the lowest common denominator. Some even claimed the relentless repetition that made Top 40 radio work was actually a form of brainwashing

Were they right?

As it turns out, the story of Todd Storz and Bill Stewart would have an interesting coda. In the wake of the Top 40 format they created, programmers finally had to respond to what people wanted to hear rather than what they thought was good for them.

As music journalist James Miller writes, "What much of the public wanted to hear was neither Chinese music nor so-called good music, but rather bluesy riffs, country reels, tricked-up pseudo-folk songs. . . . As Top 40 spread, melodies gave way to riffs, riffs became 'jingles,' jingles became 'hooks'—instantly recognizable sound patterns, either melodic or rhythmic, designed to snare a listener's attention."

Eventually one of the new breed of programmer–disc jockeys who sprang up in the wake of the new format—a man named Alan Freed—decided the streamlined blend of blues, country, folk, and pop that had emerged to serve the demands of the Top 40 audience needed a name.

The DJ called this new form of music rock and roll.

We often think of repetition and radical simplification as synonymous with dumbing things down. At its most extreme, we use terms like "mass hypnosis," "mind numbing," and "brainwashing" to describe their effects. As with all hype, however, repetition and radical simplification are not inherently negative. Music—along with prayers, mantras, proverbs, chants, and cheers—can provide comfort, relief, and excitement, depending on the context. Like the radio executives whose innovation led to Top 40 radio and rock 'n' roll, applying a healthy dose of repetition and simplification to your creative endeavors will help you burn them into the hearts and minds of those you want to reach.

Putting It into Practice

- Develop a simple slogan people can associate with you. What you need is an easy-to-remember, future-focused word bomb (think "Tune in, turn on, drop out" or "Make America Great Again"). If you're having trouble coming up with something, use literary devices. Rhymes. Alliteration. Metaphors.
- Produce a visual symbol that stands for you and what you do. Make it bold, simple, and easy to reproduce. There are plenty of designers offering their services on freelancer sites that can do this for you relatively inexpensively.
- Embrace repetition. Pinpoint the real estate your potential followers visit most frequently—online and offline. Get your slogans and symbols in front of people who frequent that real estate over and over.

EMBRACE THEATER
AND DRAMA

All business is show business.

—JAN CARLZON

Aimee Semple McPherson was the most successful preacher of
her day—if you define success by the number of people paying
attention to her and the number of dollars she brought in. She
provided the template for modern televangelists and megachurch
pastors like Joel Osteen, Pat Robertson, and Rick Warren. But
before McPherson found God, she had wanted to be an actress.
Her religious fanatic mother put the kibosh on that idea, and
McPherson dedicated herself to spreading the Good Word.

Prior to founding her world-famous Foursquare Church in
Los Angeles, McPherson traveled across the country in the 1920s

trying to make her mark. Living during that time, she faced plenty of challenges to her ambition, not the least of which was that she was a woman. On her way to the western United States (from her birthplace of Ontario, Canada), she ended up, at a certain point, in Lake Forest, Illinois. It was there she founded a church that would eventually give her the launchpad to bigger—and more lucrative—endeavors in the Golden State.

A few days after she arrived in Lake Forest, McPherson dragged a chair to a busy street corner, stood on it, and struck a rigid pose. Soon people started to gather. She remained frozen and silent. More and more people came to see the woman who looked as if she had fallen into a cataleptic trance. Some tried to rouse her. Some began to worry. Some called others over to look. Still, she remained where she was.

It was disturbing. It was strange. But the crowd stuck around. People had to see what would happen.

Then, suddenly, she snapped out of her stupor. She cried out, "Quick, follow me!" And she darted off in a straight-line shot. The crowd followed her as if her trance had been transmitted to them.

She ran through the front door of the local mission hall. The now large crowd went right though the same door. She preached her first sermon to them soon thereafter and kept that congregation for as long as she remained in Lake Forest.

Theater as we know it emerged in Athens during the sixth century BCE from its roots in a religious ritual dedicated to the god Dionysus. To the ancient Greeks, it was not mere entertainment. As a society that valued rationality and control over all else, Athenians saw the need to provide a valve through which citizens could periodically release their most primal emotions. At the same time, the city fathers viewed drama as a powerful mechanism for getting the citizenry to open up to challenging ideas and beliefs.

In Aimee Semple McPherson's time, there was no shortage of fiery preachers standing on street corners railing loudly about heaven and damnation. Following their lead would have been like putting up another flashing sign in Times Square. Instead, McPherson set herself apart using two key facets of drama—*tension* and *mystery*.

According to a BBC article on the fundamental elements of drama, "Tension is a growing sense of expectation within the drama, a feeling that the story is building up towards something happening. Without tension in a scene it is hard to keep the audience engaged with what is happening so the work may be flat and dull." It is this ability to remove the flat and the dull that gives theatricality its power, even when applied far beyond the boundaries of the stage.

So much of our lives is predictable. Of course, all of us receive our fair share of unexpected jolts (some more than others), but for the most part—especially in our bubble-wrapped modern reality—we know what we're going to encounter day in and day out. Our shock when a world-shaking event occurs—like a pandemic or economic collapse—is indicative of how unfamiliar we are with these kinds of events compared with what our ancestors experienced throughout most of their lives.

Eric Hoffer was a dock worker who spent all his free time reading about and studying what made people join mass movements and dedicate their lives to them. He published his findings in a short volume called *The True Believer*, which President Eisenhower would eventually cite as one of his favorite books. One of Hoffer's great insights was that those who cling to and spread new movements with the most feverish intensity tend not to be, as many of us believe, the poorest and most hopeless elements of our society. Rather, it is those who regularly experience persistent, unrelieved boredom that are the most easily drawn to new religions, new political movements, and new causes.

McPherson gave parishioners a way out of their boredom by ratcheting up the mystery (*Why did this stranger appear like this?*) and tension (*When is she going to finally move?*).

If you go to see a play (or watch a movie or TV show), and you figure out the ending a quarter of the way in, you probably won't recommend it to your friends. The same holds true for any movement. The same holds true for religions that take off. The same holds true in business.

Ask yourself honestly, How often do you surprise your clients, customers, or prospects?

Fortunately, you don't need to stand on a street corner to do so.

Try thinking of the least expected point of view related to your field. For instance, if most people in your space are touting authenticity, can you come up with a compelling reason to embrace artifice? If "outside-the-box thinking" is what everyone in your industry is talking about, ask yourself: "What if we thought *inside* the box?" If you're in manufacturing, are you able to conceive of some benefits to being more *inefficient* than everyone else?

For a long time, it was taken as a given that making better software was a function of programming it to do more. If you were designing a new word processing software, spreadsheet tool, or project management system, you would work to give it additional features and functions. Why would anyone, the thinking went, want to buy a tool that did *less*?

The founders of a web development company called 37signals saw things differently. Jason Fried and David Heinemeier Hansson developed a project management tool called Basecamp for their internal use. When clients began asking to buy it for their own purposes, Fried and Hansson shifted into selling Basecamp full-time.

Today Basecamp is one of most popular and lucrative pieces of software in its category. And it has fewer features than almost any other comparable product on the market.

From very early on, Fried and Hansson promoted a philosophy of technology and business as something that could be an antidote to the prevailing givens in their industry, which they felt caused great harm. In a tech-startup world in which six-day weeks and 10-hour days were viewed as the easy way out, the founders preached streamlined, efficient work schedules. They followed through by giving their teams every Friday off in the summer. In the midst of a climate where falling asleep at your desk was a badge of honor, Fried and Hansson encouraged their employees to work at home (years before catastrophic global events made it a necessity). And as we've already discussed, they advocated for technology that had a few strong features and functions rather than always adding more with each update.

The founders of 37signals (later renamed Basecamp after their main product) created drama by promoting bold views that were the opposite of what everyone in their orbit was likely to expect. They blogged about their views, gave interviews about them, and wrote books about them. With everything they published, readers wondered what these guys were going to say next. Fried and Hansson embraced their roles as gremlins in the machine. If there was a sacred cow, they found it, slaughtered it, and ate it with a generous helping of A.1. Sauce. As a result, word about their ideas, and products embodying those ideas, spread like crazy.

By all accounts, Fried and Hansson believed everything they said. But the partners were also consistent in their roles as provocateurs. They kept people guessing. They made people angry.

They generated mystery and tension.

HOLDING BACK

In the mid-seventies, a rash of posters appeared on lampposts and construction sites all over New York City's Lower East Side. On them were printed, in a ghoulish cartoon font, a single phrase:

PUNK IS COMING!

At the time these posters appeared, "punk" did not have its current connotation. It was a word that, for most people, conjured gangsters and prison talk. And that was one of the reasons the posters almost immediately generated chatter and buzz. What was *this* "punk?" Why was it coming? Who was it coming for?

When it finally got out that *Punk* was a magazine, people in the publisher's target audience of downtown bohemians snatched it up the moment it became available. It soon became so influential that it would lend its name to an entire subculture and genre of music.

Roughly around the same time, a hospital sprang up in the town of Cleveland, Georgia, seemingly out of nowhere. It was called BabyLand General. There were nurses, cribs, and incubators. But rather than live babies, every crib and incubator held a dimpled, puffy-faced doll, each of which was available for "adoption."

The dolls were called Little People and were an immediate local hit. By the 1980s, founder Xavier Roberts had changed the name to Cabbage Patch Kids. And Cabbage Patch Kids became, famously, the biggest toy phenomenon the world had ever seen.

According to the official (and endlessly promoted) narrative, Roberts had, as a child, discovered the kids in a magical cabbage patch behind a rainbow. He built BabyLand General Hospital to nurture them until they could find homes with loving families. Every kid was unique—with differences in hair, skin, facial expression, dimple position, and so on.

Cabbage Patch Kids sparked runs on store shelves and even caused riots. I was alive during the time and remember it well. Yet I never recall hearing that Xavier Roberts was an art student with entrepreneurial ambitions or that the dolls' individuality was made possible by the recent development of computerized assembly-line processes that allowed for randomized customization. That would have killed the mystery.

The trend today among marketing gurus is to advise people to put everything out there all the time. Always include your web address so people know where to find you. Always include a call to action on every email you send out so people know what they will get if they "Click here." And always make sure people can find you and your bio on LinkedIn, Facebook, Twitter, Instagram, and TikTok.

There's certainly a time and place for all this. But not *every* time and *every* place.

Can you imagine what the "Punk Is Coming" posters would have looked like with "www.punkmagazine.com" on the bottom? Do you think it would have been more effective if kids everywhere had had access to Xavier Roberts's professional résumé?

Sometimes it pays to hold back. Let people wonder what you do at first. Keep them in the dark about how to reach you, so when they finally find out, it will come as a delicious relief. Mystery builds anticipation. Anticipation builds desire. And desire ultimately creates sales.

MASTERING THE ART OF STAGING

Amway has annual revenues of close to $9 billion and operates in more than a hundred countries. The company makes so much money that it has a major sports arena named after it. And yet

Amway's individual products have only a fraction of the brand recognition of those produced by their biggest competitors. Compared with Tide, Red Bull, and Binaca, Amway's SA8 laundry detergent, XS Energy Drinks, and Sweet Shot breath spray are simply not household names.

This is not a shortcoming. It actually speaks to the sophistication of Amway's marketing. Instead of trying to compete head-to-head with the gargantuan ad budgets of consumer product holding companies like Procter & Gamble and Unilever, Amway invented "multilevel marketing"—a structure in which revenue is driven by a series of contract sales representatives who recruit other contract sales representatives, with each recruiter getting a percentage of the money brought in by all the salespeople underneath them. And to ensure their sales reps maintain the level of excitement and fervor needed to play their roles, they rely on theatrical staging.

At a typical Amway rally (of which there are many), hordes of sales reps file into an amphitheater an hour before the programmed event begins. Loud music fills the hall, while huge video screens flash slogans and symbols in time with the beat. Excitement grows as the rows fill up. At once, a seemingly spontaneous chant emerges from the crowd. One contingent in the crowd shouts "Ain't it great!" Another answers "Ain't it though!" The chants build, working the crowd into a frenzy.

Right as the anticipation of the crowd peaks and threatens to tip over into impatience, the featured event begins in earnest. The host and hostess emerge onstage, and those in the crowd who are not already standing spring to their feet, and a standing ovation explodes across the venue. This pattern continues throughout the evening.

What makes the event so fascinating from a mass psychology perspective is the discrepancy between the perception of spontaneity that the events engender in their participants and the reality of how much choreography is involved.

For example, high-level leaders of their downlines stand in strategic positions in the aisles and rows near the members of their groups to make sure they rise to their feet at the right moments. Those who don't comply are informed how bad this makes their group look, and the misstep hardly ever occurs more than once.

The light, the sound, and the us-versus-them dynamic (see Hype Strategy #1) combine to create a powerful effect. When speakers ascend the lectern to paint pictures of the sports cars and banquets and mansions that reps will obtain if they only work the program longer and harder, the emotional resonance of this heaven on earth is near impossible to resist. The net result of attending one of these rallies is that the audience members emerge with a renewed sense of fanatical energy around going out and making their dreams come true through the Amway system and worldview.

Amway is massive, and so are the theatrical spectacles the company creates. But staging doesn't have to be massive to be effective.

Real estate agents are masters of small-scale staging. They understand that while people talk about houses as if they have innate value, potential buyers who are allowed to see a property as it is normally lived in will not be willing to pay as much for it. This is why the most effective agents spend a great deal of time creating theatrical illusions. They use lighting, drapery, perfectly arranged place settings, new artwork—whatever it takes—to generate a dreamlike vision of what domestic life could be like if the buyer were to choose this and only this new home. Everyone involved understands logically that it's an illusion, including the prospective buyer. But the subconscious still cannot resist the dream.

Be conscious of staging, no matter what circles you play in. Of course, many of us already do this on a basic level. We make sure to meet clients at our offices (if we have them) instead of a park bench. We might invite important connections to a fancy restaurant instead of a local diner, even if the latter would make more sense for our present financial condition. But most of us are not anywhere near as conscious or consistent as we should be in approaching this vital art.

When you do a Zoom call with a client, how much thought do you give to what will show up in the background? If the cluttered spare room you use for a home office is what the person on the other end sees, does that project success and competence? In fact, have you even thought about what you're trying to convey through the environment you allow people to find you in?

If you're in a creative business and the artwork you surround yourself with in your office is whatever boring stock abstract print the interior decorator picked out, what do you think that says about the originality of your tastes?

If you work in an industry where there have recently been some high-profile cases of unethical behavior, is meeting clients in an office full of harsh florescent lighting and cellblock-gray cubicle partitions the wisest choice?

In business, we need to drive people to take certain actions on a regular basis. When customers or clients or partners don't buy from us or back out of a deal, they usually provide logical reasons. They say they can't afford it, or the timing isn't right, or it's "not a good fit." The real reasons for their decision, however, almost always happen well below the level of awareness.

You can shift this dynamic back in your direction through the use of staging. Theater people have understood this for eons.

Hype artists have understood it for ages. Many businesspeople still don't. This gives you an advantage.

Seize it.

ALTERNATING DOSES OF PLEASURE AND PAIN

Over the course of his career, Tony Robbins has provided coaching to Fortune 500 CEOs and US presidents, has given countless multiday seminars where he speaks nonstop for 10 hours at a stretch, and has taught millions on topics ranging from relationships to money. His reputation has recently taken a hit in many quarters in the wake of a negative chain of events beginning with a public confrontation with a defender of the #MeToo movement. However, regardless of how you feel about him as a leader, coach, or public figure, it is hard to deny his ability to get attention and drive enthusiasm among his followers. His rallies, loud gravelly voice, and weird sideways clapping all play a part in creating an addictive persona. But of all his theatrical tricks of the trade, it is arguably his fire walks for which he is best known.

Robbins claims the objective of his seminars is to break down his participants' mental patterns so they can emerge as ultraconfident beings with the power to achieve their greatest dreams. It is in this spirit that his seminar participants strip off their shoes and socks and march barefoot over a track of burning-hot coals.

If you ever get the opportunity to talk to a Tony Robbins fan who has attended one of these seminars, ask them about their firewalking experience. I've done so, and the descriptions I've received invariably sound like something akin to a religious conversion.

The level of intensity I encountered during these discussions interested me so much that I researched what might be really going on. In doing so, I happened upon an academic paper aptly called "Fire-Walking and the Brain: The Physiology of High-Arousal Rituals," written by a cognitive scientist named Dimitris Xygalatas. Not only does this obscure study explain a lot about why Tony Robbins places so much emphasis on fire walking, but it also contains lessons for people who need to build a following and get members of said following to buy from them (again and again and again).

The primary subject of Xygalatas's study is a community of Orthodox Christians in the Greek village of Agia Eleni. The group is called the Anastenaria, and for hundreds of years, it has held a Festival of the Two Saints, which many in the mainstream church have condemned as heretical.

During the festival, the Anastenaria engage in a week of religious processions, music, and ecstatic dancing. Then comes the main event. Devout participants clutch icons, strip off their shoes, and walk over a track of burning-hot coals—often scalding the soles of their feet in the process. Despite the pain and cost involved, the event's popularity has grown every year, with people from all over Greece descending on Agia Eleni to take part.

The event's strange appeal has attracted the attention of researchers, and a number of them have interviewed participants over the years. Xygalatas reviewed this body of research. As a result of doing so, he concluded that "many of [the participants] perform fire-walking without any specific reason, but later come up with an explanation for it."

Xygalatas categorizes fire walking as a high-arousal ritual, which he describes as an experience that "can stimulate the production of endogenous substances in the human body . . . [and] can lead to increased release of endorphins. Endorphins can affect emotion and motivation." High-arousal rituals also increase the production of dopamine—the brain chemical associated with craving and addiction.

By persuading someone to take part in a high-arousal ritual, a leader can literally stimulate the production of mind-altering chemicals. Furthermore, these brain chemicals benefit the leader above anyone else. As Xygalatas explains, "Endorphins can produce subjective rewards on a brain level, and dopamine can invest them with a feeling of significance. . . . This in turn provides participants with sufficient motivation to maintain and transmit the ritual."

In other words, fire walking makes people feel they are involved in something life-changing, whether or not any change ever actually takes place.

There's an old maxim about what a writer has to do to craft a compelling piece of fiction: "Put your characters up in a tree and throw rocks at them." As professionals, we often assume our efforts should be aimed at making people feel better, but the most magnetic professionals learn to seed the pleasure they deliver with doses of discomfort.

When Andy Warhol threw his Exploding Plastic Inevitable event in 1966, an immersive multimedia happening that inspired much of what would become known as club culture, he would continually observe how the crowd was responding to the music, strobe lights (the event was the first to use them in such a setting), and live performances. If he noticed the crowd simply enjoying themselves for any extended stretch, he would immediately introduce a discordant sound into the mix.

Warhol knew that if his event delivered only fun and relaxation, attendees would forget about it soon after they went home. It would lack the dramatic tension that would keep them wanting to come back for more. Pleasure is anesthetizing. A mix of tension, discomfort, and a little bit of pain keeps people focused; it gets them hooked.

This concept applies well beyond the worlds of art and entertainment. Think about top keynote speakers—the ones who get hired to give presentations for the biggest fees at the most prominent conferences and get the fattest Fortune 100 consulting gigs. Regardless of their subject matter, these professional "thought leaders" invariably inject whatever constructive or inspirational messages they are there to convey with doses of doom.

The world is changing faster than ever before, and only a few of us will be able to keep up.

Look at yourself in the mirror if you want to understand the source of your problems.

Technology will make millions of jobs obsolete. If you don't do what I say, one of them will be yours.

All these sentiments serve to make you squirm before relieving the tension.

If it is hard for you to develop this habit, reframe the concept. Remember that inflicting this kind of pain is something your customers, clients, and prospects want you to do, even if they don't know it.

CASTING AND DIRECTING

We each see ourselves as the protagonist in our own drama. Whether we realize it or not, we go through life picturing ourselves overcoming obstacles to reach our goals, battling adversaries, and aligning ourselves with great causes. And we do all of this in the eyes of some unseen audience that judges our action on how it plays out in the grand scheme of things.

If you think getting people to buy your products and services is difficult, imagine what it takes to get thousands (or millions) of people to willingly sacrifice their lives for an abstract cause. Yet that is what certain charismatic political leaders have been able to do throughout much of history.

To get to the bottom of this phenomenon, Eric Hoffer studied the radio speeches Winston Churchill made during World War II. As Hoffer describes it, "The people of London acted heroically under a hail of bombs because Churchill cast them in the role of heroes. They played their heroic role before a vast audience—ancestors, contemporaries, and posterity—and on a stage lighted by a burning world city and to the music of barking guns and screaming bombs."

Instead of crafting logical arguments, hype artists unfurl great tableaus of conflict, heroism, courage, belonging, and meaning. And while the lights and bombast and framing of theater are sure to help, the best among them can make it happen with words alone.

According to Steve Jobs, being a Mac owner wasn't just about having a better computer—it was about choosing a life of creative artistry in opposition to the gray hordes of consumer culture. In Gary Vaynerchuk's view, entrepreneurship isn't just about finding a way to make a living and controlling your time; it is a quest to prove wrong all the teachers and bosses who are constantly trying to make you settle for a life of mediocrity. And of course, Amway isn't about selling detergent and breath freshener to friends and neighbors. It is about becoming part of a grand drama in the cause of self-sufficiency.

Identify your own grand cause, your own great drama. If one doesn't already exist, invent it. This is the essence of theater. It is also the essence of hype.

Putting It into Practice

- Build anticipation whenever circumstances allow. Rather than blurt an answer out when people ask you a question, refrain for a few brief moments. Not only will this help you come up with better answers; it will lend you an air of mystery that will attract people to you.
- Pay attention to staging. Whether you are speaking to an audience of hundreds, hosting a virtual meeting, or meeting with a new connection for lunch, plan your setting and choose your props.
- Make your prospects, customers, followers, or fans a bit uncomfortable. In the midst of all you do to make them happy, inject a few "hard truths" they "need to hear."

SET DOWN A ROCK FOR YOUR FOLLOWERS TO CLING TO

And I say also unto thee that thou art Peter,
and on this rock I will build my church.

—JESUS OF NAZARETH

Lafayette Ronald Hubbard was in a bad place. He had entered the Navy at the peak of the Second World War, expecting an experience that mirrored the heroic deeds he wrote about for a penny a word at the pulp magazines from which he made his living. But his over-the-top personality did not make the desired impression on his senior officers. Instead of commanding a fleet tasked with liberating Europe from the Nazi menace, the junior lieutenant found himself in charge of a PC-815 craft with the unglamorous mission of patrolling the coast of Southern California.

Although the first few months at his new post were as lack-luster as he had feared, one evening he detected some unusual blips on the ship's sonar. Contrary to the advice of a number of experienced shipmates, he commanded the crew to fire on the underwater vessels, convinced he was defending the home front from an imminent invasion. After 68 straight hours of "combat," he learned that a magnetic deposit in the area was what was causing the reading. Hubbard received a severe reprimand and was relieved of his command. He ended the war in an infirmary, suffering from pains undoubtedly related more to emotional stress than to anything sustained in battle.

As he reintegrated into civilian life, things only got worse for Hubbard. His specialty as a pulp fiction writer was space opera, a subgenre of science fiction particularly well suited to his ability to make up outlandish scenarios. Before the war, Hubbard's ability to churn out thousands of words at a sitting had allowed him to eke out an income. Now his ability to conjure plots on demand seemed to have abandoned him. He took out large loans, which he had no means of paying back, and was arrested for financial malfeasance. His marriage deteriorated.

Hubbard had always felt himself to be destined for greatness, but now he had no money, no real family life, and no reputation. But then, over the course of a few months, everything changed. By the start of the next decade, Hubbard was rich, famous, and adored.

What had happened to so dramatically reverse Hubbard's half-decade downward slide?

In May 1950, L. Ron Hubbard—as he became known—released *Dianetics: The Modern Science of Mental Health*. The book claimed to offer a revolutionary system that regular human beings could use to reach their full potential and significantly improve every area of their lives. Hubbard had no formal education in psychology or philosophy, but the book drew heavily on both. It also included a slew of vague but impressive case studies detailing instances in which he had used his system to help down-and-out subjects to become nearly superhuman.

The psychiatric community rejected Hubbard's methods and claims. The absence of scientific verification of his work, in the form of hard data or double-blind testing, was a particular sticking point. Once in a while, a skeptical layperson would ask him to produce one of the book's success stories in the flesh, but he had a knack for deflecting these sorts of questions with an entertaining quip or anecdote.

In the end, none of it mattered.

The book was a smash. It remained on the *New York Times* bestseller list for 28 weeks and sold 18 million copies. People formed Dianetics groups throughout the country to attempt to get a sliver of this life-changing power for themselves. Between royalties, speaking fees, and revenues from the training centers, his wealth skyrocketed.

As for what came next—well, many of us are familiar with that part. Hubbard went on to found the Church of Scientology, a religion that has since attracted many thousands of followers, including Tom Cruise, John Travolta, Kirstie Alley, and Elisabeth Moss. While Scientology has experienced its fair share of controversy, the financial value to its founder was unambiguous. At the time of his death in 1986, L. Ron Hubbard's personal net worth was $60 million. The organization is still going strong.

What L. Ron Hubbard managed to accomplish, beginning with *Dianetics*, was to present a system to which people could look for answers in the face of any one of life's dilemmas, trials, and challenges. He understood the void (see Hype Strategy #7) and had a knack for filling it.

Life is inherently uncertain. Regardless of whatever fore-thought, planning, or second-guessing any of us might engage in, we will all eventually get knocked down by tragedy, misfortune, or random accident. We invest in relationships, only to have the objects of our desire reject us or leave us. We open our hearts to family members, only to have them die. We work hard and follow the advice of wise mentors, only to lose our jobs and have our businesses fail. At a certain point, we are all confronted with the reality that nothing is permanent. We ultimately watch what we care about go away or fall apart for no good reason.

For many of us (maybe even most of us), this bleak reality is too difficult to accept. It is one thing to go through hard times, but to go through hard times knowing there is nothing consistent on which we can rely feels unbearable.

This presents an opportunity for the hype artist. If you are able to create something that appears solid and unchangeable—something that provides answers or comfort or guidance in every situation no matter how hard things get—those you provide it to will follow you anywhere.

In 1986, an engineer at Motorola named Bill Smith developed a process improvement methodology, which he named Six Sigma. The methodology spread and was eventually adopted by General Electric CEO Jack Welch, who regularly touted its benefits in pub-lic. Before long, businesses of every size and type were declaring themselves as Six Sigma organizations, and managers at every level were prominently displaying their Six Sigma credentials.

At its peak, it was common in the corporate world to refer every matter back to Six Sigma principles. The ubiquity of the methodology was even parodied by Alec Baldwin on the NBC sitcom 30 Rock, where he played a top executive who constantly talked about his "Six Sigma Black Belt Ultra."

Corporate culture can be unforgiving. Despite platitudes about "failing fast" and "radical transparency," making mistakes and accepting responsibility for setbacks will often lead to lost status or job loss. While Six Sigma is useful in many ways, it is far from the one and only solution to every business problem. Its greatest value resided in giving managers and executives a comprehensive explanation for every decision they made, which they could point to in times of uncertainty.

In this regard, Six Sigma was not too different from the scripture to which priests refer to explain acts of God. If you can manage to create and control the most relevant "scripture" in your space, your ability to amass power over those who rely on it will be incredible. The trick is to figure out what form that scripture should take in order to give it the most pull and widest reach possible.

PRODUCE A BIBLE

When Madame Helena Blavatsky, the Russian aristocrat (if that's what she actually was), immigrated to the United States during the late nineteenth century, a circle of dedicated students gathered around her regularly to hear her pontificate on her new philosophy. She was charismatic, confident, and mysterious—regaling her small group of followers with stories of letters written from invisible overlords, conversations with spirits, and previously unknown ancient civilizations.

While her students adored her, it wasn't enough. Blavatsky wanted money, fame, and influence. And she knew making that happen was going to require a whole different level of hype.

You see, Madame Blavatsky was entering into a space with a ton of competition. In the wake of the Fox sisters, mediums claiming to have the power to communicate with the dead flooded the market, bringing all kinds of cobbled-together spiritual systems with them.

So how did Blavatsky set herself apart to the public at large?

She wrote a bible.

In many business circles, it has become commonplace to talk about how important it is to publish (or self-publish) a book to establish yourself as an expert. There is a lot of wisdom in this advice—to a point. For most of human history, it has been incredibly hard to get ideas into writing. Paper, ink, printing, and distribution were all expensive in terms of time and effort. As a result, literate cultures developed traditions and institutions to ensure that if something was going to be printed, it had to be of the highest quality.

At the same time, not all books are created equal. When a book is overly tactical—or technical—readers may see it as a helpful resource, but not as an all-encompassing source of authority.

That's why Madame Blavatsky didn't produce a book called *How to Conduct a Winning Séance* or *Innovative Spiritual Strategies for the 19th Century*. Instead she published *Isis Unveiled*, a book claiming to have finally and definitely unlocked all the secrets of how the universe actually worked.

It was an immediate bestseller. It wasn't a coincidence that her rise as the leader of a worldwide movement followed soon after.

Likewise, *Dianetics* doesn't only give advice and tips on how to improve oneself. It is presented as the one and only blueprint for anyone who wants to live a fulfilling life. For example, on the second page of that book, Hubbard writes that "Dianetics is an exact science and its application is on the order of, but simpler than, engineering. Its axioms should not be confused with theories since they demonstrably exist as natural laws hitherto undiscovered."

A few pages later, it refers to the system as the culmination of all earlier forms of knowledge, claiming that it "deals with facts rather than theories" and that "an exact science [like Dianetics] does not 'believe' but establishes and proves facts."

In Chapter 3 of *Dianetics*, Hubbard walks his readers through a brief history of humankind's various attempts to figure out an all-encompassing view of how the mind works, referring to the efforts as scattered pieces of an incomplete jigsaw puzzle. *Dianetics*, on the other hand, is the completed puzzle, available at last. Hubbard repeatedly refers to his system as a "science" (see Hype Strategy #8), while leaving out any actual science that might get in the way.

What distinguishes the scientific method from other ways of understanding the world is that it is willing to accept the wrongness of its own principles and discoveries based on new evidence. *Dianetics*, on the other hand, essentially says: "Look no further; everything you ever needed to know about perfecting your state of mind is within these pages." It offers security instead of uncertainty, while cloaking itself in scientific jargon.

Exquisite hype.

L. Ron Hubbard literally founded a new religion around his book. So did Madame Helena Blavatsky (she called it Theosophy). That's not entirely necessary, though. Many of the most successful self-help and business gurus out there write and publish books. The business and personal development books that have truly transformed the careers of their authors—*Think and Grow Rich* by Napoleon Hill, *How to Win Friends and Influence People* by Dale Carnegie, *The Secret* by Rhonda Byrne, and *The 4-Hour Workweek* by Tim Ferriss, for example—provide a comprehensive explanation of how all things in their corner of the universe work.

These books promise—implicitly and sometimes explicitly—that if you want to understand everything there is to know about gaining power, accumulating wealth, building relationships, or becoming productive and efficient, there is no need to look anywhere other than between their pages. As such, their authors attain an almost magical aura.

To create your own bible, begin by writing down your own beliefs about the way the world works. We all have these. Even if we aren't religious, or don't follow some particular school of thought, we all have a personal philosophy cobbled together from our upbringing, various experiences and encounters we've had, and advice we've received. We use this philosophy as a benchmark to guide our decision-making, although we often don't articulate to ourselves what this philosophy is.

Now is the time to clarify your own personal philosophy to yourself. If you didn't have to worry about what other people thought, or worry about your own self-image of being a fair and balanced person, what would you say you believe?

People never change?

Life is a relentless competition for status?

Creativity is mystical?

Whatever these beliefs are, get them down. They will form the foundation of your bible. Present each one as a universal truth that your readers can follow—step-by-step and beat-by-beat—to guide the course of their lives. Whether you write up your collected beliefs by yourself or have someone do it for you and put your name on it, you will end up with a bible.

CREATE A CHURCH

Once you have a bible, it is time to start a church.

Starting a church is the best growth hacking method ever invented. A 2005 *Economist* article on the megachurch phenomenon states: "The best churches (like some of the most notorious cults) have discovered the secret of low-cost and self-sustaining growth; transforming seekers into evangelicals who will then go out and recruit more seekers."

This strategy doesn't only work for religious institutions—mega or otherwise. If you give people any kind of ready-made label and set of beliefs, they will go to great lengths to get others to join the tribe. And since every tribe has a chief, this puts you as founder in an enviable position.

Sometime in the late fifties, a mediocre college-level golfer named Mark McCormack realized that he would have a better chance at success if he stopped trying to become a pro and started representing those who had a real shot. In college, he had crossed paths with a fellow golfer named Arnold Palmer and recognized his ability. When McCormack graduated, he founded a company called International Management Group, or IMG—a sports agency that existed solely to represent Arnold Palmer.

Palmer ended up becoming one of the best players to ever pick up a club (not to mention his talent for inventing nonalcoholic drinks). It was an auspicious start for the upstart agency. But what really set McCormack and his company apart from other sports agents was where he went next.

In 1968, Mark McCormack decided that what golf needed was a comprehensive system of player rankings.

Buoyed by his first-mover advantage, he presented his system as the single standard by which golfers would henceforth be judged.

McCormack's formula, which was ostensibly based on some mathematical algorithm, quickly became recognized as the arbiter of quality in a player's game, rather than any number of other possible benchmarks, such as, say, how many games a player won.

Case in point: According to the IMG's ranking system, pro golfer Lee Westwood only had a world ranking of number 6, even though he had gone on an unparalleled streak of 11 wins in 34 tournaments.

A few cynics raised some fuss, citing the inconvenient fact that Westwood wasn't a client of IMG. But the noncontroversy came and went. Why? Because in a sport like golf, which is full of nonuniform courses and handicaps, the ranking system provides certainty. It is a clear set of standards issued by an authority in the field presented with utter confidence and backed by an organization.

By establishing his system as *the* mechanism for determining good, bad, and everything in between, McCormack positioned IMG as the ultimate authority in the game of golf. As I define it, a church is an organized grouping whose members share a common identification based on a shared belief in a source of authority and certainty. The Ten Commandments are the source of all moral authority. The answers to all your questions about how we got here can be found in the pages of Genesis. The way to eliminate suffering is to follow the Eightfold Path. Confession and Communion are a way into heaven even after you've sinned. The way to become an effective manufacturer, regardless of how complex the situation, is to measure production according to the mathematic principles of scientific management. Cutting taxes is the cure to any economic malady.

Katharine Cook Briggs—eventually joined by her daughter, Isabel Briggs Myers—created the Myers-Briggs Type Indicator

(MBTI), despite (like L. Ron Hubbard) having no academic training in psychology, sociology, or science of any kind. To create the assessment, Briggs read a bunch of biographies of famous people. From this, she grouped every single person on earth into 16 categories and called it law.

Echoing the sentiments of countless mainstream psychologists, University of Pennsylvania's Adam Grant writes, "There's no evidence behind [the MBTI]. The characteristics measured by the test have almost no predictive power." Even so, roughly 2 million people per year take the test, and many of the world's largest companies, including $10 billion-plus consulting giant McKinsey & Company, continue to administer (and pay for) it.

Once a rock is set down, it is incredibly difficult to dislodge.

There are many forms your church, your bible . . . your rock . . . can take. You can develop your own assessment. You can create a manifesto—a list of declarative statements your followers can refer to whenever they are unsure about what to do. You can invent a three-pronged formula or a six-step system.

While the details of your rock are certainly important, what matters most is that your followers perceive it as the key to unlocking every puzzle they will even encounter in their work or in their lives. Understanding shades of gray might be useful for developing an accurate view of reality, but those who wish to amass influence must learn to traffic in the black and white. Many hype artists hawking thinly researched theories and barely tested cures have derived great benefit from this strategy. If you apply it to something worthwhile, the potential is limitless.

- Document your beliefs about the way the world works. Present a manifesto that describes how followers can get what they want out of life—step-by-step and beat-by-beat.
- Start your church—an organized grouping whose members share a common identification based on a shared belief in a source of authority and certainty. It can take the form of an institution or club.
- Create an assessment. Group people into categories. If you can give people a tool that allows them to define their own identities, they will keep coming back for more. It is easy to build such an assessment now using any of the online quiz-creation platforms out there.

FETISHIZE WORK, MASTER EFFORTLESS DOING

Through actionless action they can make the whole world
do as they will and yet not be wearied.

—CHUANG TZU

Gary Vaynerchuk produces a ton of material in the form of videos, articles, books, and podcasts dedicated to the subject of how important it is to constantly hustle. According to this flood of media, he regularly stays up until three in the morning, sending and responding to emails to cement connections. He spends every spare minute he has on social media—in between meetings, in cars, during commercials, and in the bathroom. And when he's not doing all that, he's creating content and running his company. Furthermore, those who are not doing this—well, that's totally their right—but they should never expect anything but a life teth-ered to a cubicle and mired in mediocrity.

Vaynerchuk first made his name, and fortune, with a project called Wine Library TV. Wine Library TV features him review-ing various wines in his signature Jersey bro style, presenting his recommendations with humor and panache. Breaking from the standard practice of talking about wines in terms of notes of blackberry meets coffee meets smokiness, Gary would compare them to flavors like Skittles and Cinnamon Toast Crunch.

By his own admission, he toiled to create content for Wine Library TV for more than a year before anyone paid atten-tion. Once he gained his first real fans, it was still a slow climb. Eventually, through relentless hard work and hustle (of course), he built a massive following for his online show—which funneled directly into sales for his online wine shop Wine Library.

According to the official version of the story, Vaynerchuk's Wine Library and Wine Library TV were responsible for turning his immigrant father's tiny liquor store into a $60 million business. What he underplays in this telling is that the liquor store already had revenues of $3 million a year. Naturally, this leads into the question of how he was able to work on Wine Library TV for a year without anyone noticing while not worrying about where the money was coming from. Well, it certainly didn't hurt that he had his father's (not so tiny) business to rely on.

Vaynerchuk's recipe for success through around-the-clock social media self-promotion runs into problems if you don't start out with a financial cushion. It also won't work quite as well if you're the one who has to make the wine instead of just selling it. So while hard work is certainly important, it is far from the only (or even the most essential) factor in what makes some people do better than others in business. It was this observation that inspired me to challenge Vaynerchuk in print, and the move certainly boosted my visibility.

In the years since, however, Vaynerchuk hasn't backed off from his message. He has kept his theme simple and repeats it relentlessly.

As he summed it up during one interview on Mashable, "If I'm more successful than you, there's one reason for it—it's because I outworked you."

Gary Vaynerchuk is no dummy. He's not the kind of person who wastes time or marketing dollars. Vaynerchuk doesn't berate his viewers, readers, and listeners for not working hard enough out of pure goodwill. He does it because it's good for business.

If there is one lesson you should take from this book, it's to stop paying so much attention to the advice that hype artists give and start modeling what they actually do. Nowhere is this truer than on the subject of work.

THE TOM SAWYER EFFECT

In *Age of Propaganda*, social psychologists Anthony Pratkanis and Elliot Aronson dedicate a lot of time to dissecting the practices of the Unification Church and its founder, Reverend Sun Myung Moon. Since 1954, the "Moonie" movement has amassed 1 million to 2 million followers. By some measures, it is considered the largest cult in the world.

What is the secret of the Unification Church's success? The answer is manifold, but its founder's and followers' relationship to work definitely plays a part. Pratkanis and Aronson observed that members of the church work, on average, 67 hours a week on behalf of the group. Most of this time is spent raising money and recruiting new members. And they do it all for free.

This is not an unusual feature of rapid-growth movements of all kinds. The leader of the nineteenth-century millenarian free love Oneida commune pushed his followers to perform huge amounts of manual labor in order to build "heaven on earth." The Church of Jesus Christ of Latter-Day Saints requires young members to dedicate two years of their lives to missions made up of 16-hour training days and six-day weeks in the field. Amway relentlessly encourages people to recruit, recruit, recruit and sell, sell, sell by "asking new members to decide on their 'Dream'—a new Cadillac, a summer cottage, a new ranch, or whatever they would like to get by selling Amway products."

Those of you who paid attention in junior high school English class might recognize the following story from the Mark Twain classic *The Adventures of Tom Sawyer*. Tom's aunt told him to paint a fence white on a beautiful summer day while the rest of his friends were goofing off and enjoying the outdoors. He really didn't feel like it. So instead of hunkering down and working hard, ol' Tom started whistling and singing so that everyone could hear him.

Soon enough, every kid in the town was whitewashing that fence. Every kid but Tom Sawyer, that is. The scene ends with Tom kicking back in the shade with his back against a tree, eating an apple, while a whole gang of kids did his job for him, thinking all the while they were doing something fun.

Promoting the idea of fulfillment, success, or salvation through toil is the cheapest and most efficient way for a hype artist to get others to spread their message for them. By reframing hustle on behalf of your cause or your product as something that will make their lives better—perhaps now but preferably in the future—you will create an army of evangelist worker bees.

When you get yourself into a situation in which two contradictory beliefs appear equally real, your mind will tell itself all kinds of stories to iron out the discrepancies. This psychological conflict is called cognitive dissonance, and it drives the way we see and interpret reality, regardless of the facts.

If you are convinced to buy into the idea that working relentlessly on behalf of a certain vision—whether for a cause or for your own advancement—and then you come across evidence suggesting it may not get you there, your brain has a hard time reconciling such a waste of time and energy. To accommodate this discomfort, most people double down. They subconsciously tell themselves to work even harder. This is one of the reasons why, by fetishizing hard work, hype artists bind their followers to them ever more tightly.

George Ivanovich Gurdjieff was a spiritual leader who garnered a large and influential following in the early twentieth century. He was a masterful mythmaker, establishing himself as a magus who, in the words of follower and fellow guru Peter Damien Ouspensky, "knew everything and could do everything."

Gurdjieff was a master of theater, leading acolytes upon their arrival to his compound through, in the words of biographer Peter Washington, "dark passages into dimly lit rooms adorned with carpets and shawls, the ceilings draped like tents in the eastern fashion, orientalia scattered round the walls . . . icons and ivory statues of Moses, Mahomet, Buddha and Christ. . . . Opposite the final door, staring straight at the visitor with penetrating but not unfriendly eyes, a silent middle aged man sat cross-legged on an ottoman smoking a water pipe."

Once Gurdjieff had attracted followers, he knew the real money was to be made in keeping them in his fold for as long as possible.

In between vague lectures on spiritual practice, the guru would make it clear that true enlightenment would not come from whatever foolish notions they had brought with them to the compound. Instead, it would come from breaking themselves down and stripping everything about themselves away until they were left with their essential selves.

To this end, Gurdjieff assigned them menial tasks.

Some of the tasks had the convenient benefit of helping beautify the home and grounds where he lived and the participants resided (for a steep fee paid to the guru, of course). Others were entirely useless. At the peak of his fame and influence, it would not be unusual to see movie stars bent over in rows on his property digging holes to nowhere. It was also not uncommon for these same movie stars to return to Gurdjieff's spiritual retreats over and over again.

Like Tom Sawyer promoting the pleasures of painting a fence in the hot sun, Gurdjieff reframed backbreaking work as a spirit-cleansing endeavor. After spending hours and days toiling to achieve enlightenment, it would have been tough for any of the participants to admit to themselves that Gurdjieff was scamming them. So they told themselves what they were doing was meaningful. And they kept forking over their dollars for the privilege of doing more of it.

Despite whatever flaws they may have possessed, Moon and Gurdjieff were natural marketers. They understood that the more they got followers to hustle, the stronger the followers' attachment to them would become.

In the world of marketing and advertising agencies, there's an old maxim you hear a lot, which says you should always "under-promise and overdeliver." In other words, you should charge for a certain amount of work and then do a lot more work than that. As a result, your clients will be happy and hire you again and again.

This advice betrays a scant understanding of human psychology.

Making a display of excessive hard work on behalf of someone else does not make them see you as indispensable. Quite the opposite. Clients may keep you around for working tirelessly on their behalf, but only if you up the effort—and the results you deliver—month over month and year after year.

Remember, people are very adaptable when change happens gradually (see Hype Strategy #4). The harder you work and the more you do for clients, the more they will expect you to do for them going forward. This isn't ingratitude; it's human nature.

Compare this relationship with the one Strategic Coach—one of the first-ever business coaching companies—has with its clients.

Today Strategic Coach is a multimillion-dollar organization with locations in Chicago, Toronto, Los Angeles, and London. The program is not cheap—I spent close to $30,000 to take part to learn how to make the shift from copywriting practice to marketing agency, and I still use a lot of what the company taught me.

When you sign up for the program, you attend an eight-hour workshop four times a year. You sit in the workshop with about 20 or 30 fellow entrepreneurs, and one instructor delivers the same information to everyone in the group at the same time. While you're certainly allowed to ask questions, the instructor keeps the schedule moving along at a gently militaristic clip, ensuring no segment extends past one of the designated breaks or the closing bell.

As for the tools, techniques, and tips we took away, these all awaited us at our desks when we arrived, on professionally printed, standardized forms, collected in uniform binders embossed with the Strategic Coach logo. Any customization that occurred within the pages of these binders came from our own minds and pens.

At designated times throughout the day, our instructor asked us to fill in the blanks on various exercises to build the specifics of our strategic plan or map of our goals or whatever was relevant at the time. Then we were told to use those self-customized tools to go out into the world and improve our businesses.

While there were a few group calls between sessions and a handful of one-on-one advisory calls with a junior-level member of the organization, the bulk of what we got for our money was those quarterly workshops. When we would reconvene after three months, our instructor would always ask us how we did in applying the tools to our businesses.

Since there was no way I was going to spend that kind of money and not use what I learned, I was more rigorous than most in using the tools we came away with. But even I wasn't perfect. Most of my classmates, especially those with more mature businesses, used the tools to a far less extent.

This made sense. Implementing the tools took a lot of time and a lot of work. However, no one ever said to the instructor, "You know, I'm paying you guys a lot of money, and you're standing there asking me if I worked hard enough using the prefabricated tools you gave me three months ago."

Instead, a look of shame would spread over their faces. They would apologize. They would talk about how in the first few weeks after they left the workshop, they were fired up to implement what they had learned. But then somehow they had slipped. They had gotten caught up with the day-to-day grind of their businesses. They had let themselves slack off. They promised to do better next time.

The instructor would allow an indulgent smile. Then she would say, "Go easy on yourself. The goal is progress, not perfection."

The relief on the faces of the client-students was palpable. They had confessed falling short of the toil required for salvation and had been forgiven.

The dynamic established by Strategic Coach was that you paid the organization handsomely to be told of all the work you need to do with the systems and materials given to you in order to be successful. If you don't do the work, it's on you.

If you can find ways to put your clients and customers to work implementing your ideas rather than always doing the implementing for them, they will keep coming back for more. On the other hand, if you do all the work for them, they will blame you when it inevitably goes wrong to any degree (and, often, even when it goes right).

ACHIEVING THE INTERNAL STATE
YOU NEED TO SUCCEED

The question remains: Do hype artists practice what they preach? Of course, many hype artists work hard on behalf of their own businesses, careers, projects, and causes. At the same time, they tend not to rush around desperate to fill every spare minute with activity. Hype artists' relationship to the work they do on their own behalf is far different from what they preach in public.

In the early pages of this book, I explained that one of the main reasons I decided to write the book was to put the tools of hype into the hands of the "good guys." While we've looked at many examples of people and organizations that have used these strategies to advance worthwhile ideas, causes, and businesses, there is no avoiding the reality that there are more "bad guys" who have mastered hype than there are those using these strategies to make the world a better place.

Why is this?

If they were to ever be subjected to a formal psychological evaluation, many of the scummiest of the scumbags we've profiled in these pages would most likely be classified under the broad diagnostic category called antisocial personality disorder (APD), which includes narcissism, psychopathy, and sociopathy.

People with APD are simply more detached than the rest of us. As cognitive scientist Kathleen Taylor describes it, "In a brain imaging study of APD and non-APD male volunteers . . . participants were given a social stressor (being asked to prepare and deliver a speech in four minutes) while researchers measured basic stress responses, such as heart rate, and the size of the prefrontal cortex. APD participants had significantly smaller prefrontal cortices and were significantly less stressed: on average, their heart rate was more than eight beats a minute slower than their non-APD peers.'"

So while their lack of empathy often wreaks havoc on their personal relationships, not to mention tearing apart the social fabric, the kinds of people who become propagandists and con artists and cult leaders tend to have the internal makeup that allows them to coolly make the moves needed to gain particular results. They can maintain the distance necessary to take deliberate action based on the world as it really is, rather than constantly reacting based on the emotions most of us have about how we wish the world could be.

No matter how hard the rest of us work, or how meticulously we plan, we constantly allow our emotions to sabotage our best efforts. We blurt out exactly the wrong thing at an important meeting. We send an angry email in a fit of pique. We spend months planning a marketing campaign and then fire off a tweet on a whim that derails the whole thing. We tense up and freak out. We back down when we should stand up and stand up when we should back down.

If any of this sounds familiar, don't be too hard on yourself. It just means you're a regular, nonsociopathic human being.

Despite our capacity for reason, most of us spend the majority of our waking hours trying to tamp down the seething emotions that afflict us at all times. We might tell ourselves we have logical reasons for doing what we do. Deep down, however, we know most of our actions are designed to make ourselves feel better, despite whether the actions in questions help us get what we want in the long run.

To combat this tendency, you must identify ways to cultivate and maintain the state of equilibrium that doesn't come built into your regular-human internal software.

Let's return for a moment to the particular breed of hype artist known as the "pickup artist." If you're troubled by the thought of hordes of young men poring over a book to learn how to manipulate women, there is a consolation. The majority of guys who bought the book by Neil Strauss (aka Style) on the subject were unable to replicate its author's results.

This is because most of them imitated Style's specific tactics in an attempt to brainwash women into coming home with them. What these failed pickup artists had trouble understanding is that the most successful seducers never try to get anyone to do what they don't want to do. Instead, they create an atmosphere that gives people a sensation of excitement and comfort, which allows them to decide for themselves whether they want to embark on a new adventure. And to do this, mastery over one's own emotional state is essential.

Even if you have been happily married for 40 years, there is a lot you can learn from these self-made lotharios about moving others to action.

At one point in *The Game*, Strauss recounts a speech that his friend and mentor Mystery gives to a group of nervous young men that he is coaching before they go to a club to try out the techniques they have just learned from him.

"All your emotions are going to try to [mess] you up," he says. "They are there to confuse you, so know right now that they cannot be trusted at all. You will feel shy sometimes, and self-conscious, and you must deal with it like you deal with a pebble in your shoe. It's uncomfortable, but you ignore it. It's not part of the equation."

Easier said than done, right?

No matter what tactics, techniques, strategies, or psychological principles you learn, you will inevitably fail to execute them unless you master your emotions. You may know exactly what you should do in any given situation, but your anxiety, fear, desire, desperation, or preconceived notions will inevitably control what you actually do.

Luckily, there is a way around this.

THE ART OF SELF-REGULATION

In Chinese philosophy, there is a concept called "wu-wei," which translates approximately into "actionless action" or "effortless doing." Taoists, in particular, view this as the optimal state from which to lead, achieve, and influence. Masters of wu-wei let everyone else rush around, work beyond their capacity, and expend themselves emotionally. Then they swoop in and get their way before anyone realizes what has happened.

The ability to self-regulate is a prerequisite for being effective at persuasion, influence, marketing, and sales. It is this self-regulation that gives us regular decent folks a shot at approximating the strategic cool that the antisocial hype artists naturally possess.

If you were to follow every strategy in this book, you would get everything you ever wanted. But you won't be able to—at least, not right away. Getting your emotions under control is the missing piece of the hype equation. It is also its most difficult piece. But if you are able to become a master of self-regulation, every word you speak, sentence you write, and action you take will have incredible influence and impact.

Each of us will have a somewhat different practice for achieving this state, depending on our inclinations and our temperaments. That said, there are a few practices that will take almost everyone closer to the optimal state for the benevolent hype artist.

THE CRAFT OF SELF-REGULATION

Emotions are physical. They have as much to do with your heart rate and cortisol levels as with your personality and upbringing. As such, much of what you need to do to regulate your emotions will be physical.

It may seem basic, but first and foremost, movement is key. And when I say movement, what I mean is vigorous exercise.

The way we live now is more sedentary than at any other time in human history or prehistory. We are evolved to live in small bands of roving hunter-gatherers who walked miles and miles every day. This state of constantly being on the move lasted many millennia longer than the state of remaining in one place that came about as a result of the development of agriculture and the birth of cities. Even over most of the last 5,000 to 8,000 years since farming became a way of life, almost everyone spent the bulk of every day engaged in some sort of physical labor.

As we encounter various challenges, we build up the stress hormone cortisol in our bloodstreams. The natural human way of dealing with the unpleasantness this buildup causes is to discharge it through physical exertion. However, with most of us engaged in office work—and spending most of our leisure time in front of screens—this discharge does not happen. As a result, we experience much of the discomfort of stress and conflict as much more intense—much more real—than it actually is. We make decisions from that frame, many of them decidedly nonstrategic.

Give yourself an advantage in this area. Find a form of physical activity that you can stand and that makes you sweat, and engage in it most days. Before I started doing this, I figured the difference would be subtle. It was not. It was incredibly dramatic.

In recent years, meditation (in the West, at least) has gone from the realm of bearded, patchouli-scented hippies to a practice embraced by Silicon Valley, Fortune 500 corporations, and neuroscientists alike. There's a good reason for this: It works. Spending time focused on your breathing and doing so regularly allows you to detach from your emotions to some degree.

The more you meditate, the more you realize the feelings welling up inside you in response to certain stimuli are simply sensations. You begin to understand how unnecessary it is to immediately react to each and every one of them. This is an incredibly helpful skill for any hype artist to have.

What you put into your body matters. This is different for each person, but there are some commonalities. Excess in any form never helps. Huge amounts of caffeine, sugar, and trans fats affect the mood and raise anxiety levels.

I know for me, when I discovered green tea and began to substitute four of my five daily cups of coffee with it, my agitation decreased, and I was better able to keep from blurting out the first thing that came to my mind in any given situation. I eventually learned green tea contains a substance called L-theanine that is absent from coffee, which calms the nervous system and promotes relaxation (it is offered in pill form as well).

Some people with more deeply entrenched blocks may need to find a good therapist.

Experiment on yourself: Try mindfulness meditation. Vigorous exercise. Clean eating. Or any of the other practices that humans have been using for eons to combat our own bombastic, impulsive natures. Find out what works for you. But do something.

We often think of our self-regulation practices as secondary—something that comes after all the work and learning is done. However, if you want your work and learning to have a real-world effect—to get you the results you want—you must put in the time to regulate the powerful sensations that originate in the physical body and physical brain.

Often, when it comes to engaging in the kinds of activities that allow us to calm our internal states and gain critical distance—whether meditation, exercise, or sleep—we try to figure out how to cram them into our already overloaded schedules. Yet if we want to successfully influence people, we need to consider these activities first.

If you have regularly sabotaged your attempts to become influential by failing to control yourself, don't worry too much about it. Most people in the world are just like you. The true test is whether you will recognize this about yourself and take the steps necessary to change it.

Putting It into Practice

- Find a way to sell your expertise without actually doing the work *for* your customers. This might be a video course or a speaking series or a seminar.
- Find a form of physical activity that you can stand and that makes you sweat, and engage in it most days.
- Implement a meditative practice. This could be traditional Eastern-style meditation, but plenty of other traditions have practices that might be more suitable to you. Whatever specific method you choose, this will help you reduce the power your emotions have over you.

EPILOGUE

Evil and conniving people manipulate, right? Wrong.
Everyone manipulates. Manipulation simply means that you
are attempting to influence other people's behavior toward your ends.
—MICHELE WEINER-DAVIS

Nobles and peasants. Kings and subjects. Fat cats and workers. Trust fund kids and kids from the projects.

A lot has changed since the bulk of *Homo sapiens* stopped roaming the savannah, but one thing has remained remarkably constant. There has never been a civilization on earth that has been truly fair. It's an unpleasant feature of our species, and one that many people have tried to explain over the years.

They tend to fall into two camps. Some place all the blame on the inherent awfulness of whatever culture happens to be dominant at any given time. According to this version of reality, history is simply a series of episodes of exploitation, theft, and oppression in which the powerful dominate the powerless. One day, the story goes, we'll finally have a revolution that will end this state of affairs. On the other side is the idea that all people have an equal opportunity to better themselves, achieve all their dreams, and become multimillionaires. If you aren't doing as well as others, it's your own fault. As long as you stay on the straight and narrow, you'll ultimately get everything you ever wanted.

Really, neither of these viewpoints is accurate. One government gets overthrown, and the replacement creates a society more unequal than the last. People work hard their whole lives and die broke anyway. Wishing the world was different does not change the circumstances. Playing the game of life according to a set of rules put in place by the people who already have all the power is the best way to get nowhere.

Fortunately, there is a tool that allows for an escape route from this predicament. Hype.

It is easy for those who sit at the center of power in a society to follow the traditional methods of getting what they want. When you grow up with the right educational opportunities, right background, right interests, right personality, and right race, it is relatively easy to make your way in the world using tried-and-true channels. But for those who exist on the fringes of that world—those without resources or connections—creating a life full of opportunity requires more unconventional methods.

Hype allows those without power to gain access to it. It provides those on the bottom the ability to leapfrog over those at the top, or at least to get where they want to go through a side door. It gives the ignored a chance to grab attention and the unconnected a chance to penetrate inner circles.

Remember back in Strategy #8 when I mentioned C Bin and Zeyu Zheng—the two young guys I interviewed for my *Forbes* column? Well, there is an interesting coda to that story. In the wake of our interview, I told them about my work on hype, and it was right up their alley. They offered to fly me over to China to speak to a group of entrepreneurs they would be training.

I agreed, but I have to admit I was nervous. At the time, I had only spoken on the subject of hype a few times before in a formal setting. While those few stateside speeches had gone relatively well, there was always one person who would start debating with me during the Q&A portion about the morality and wisdom of what I was teaching.

"I get this stuff you're telling us about how manipulating people can be effective. But isn't it better to just put your message out there and let the cream rise to the top?"

Or . . .

"What if I don't want to be the kind of person who uses these kinds of tactics?"

Or . . .

"Why do you call it hype? Doesn't that have, like, a negative connotation?"

I'd always get into a bit of a back-and-forth with these naysayers, and they would usually nod their heads politely. But I could always tell they didn't buy it. And this was in the United States of

America—a country literally founded on the belief that you should do whatever you need to do in the "pursuit of happiness."

Now I was going to deliver the same message to an audience in a country that was known for its collective spirit. I had always heard that people in China prized rules over rebellion, solidarity over standing out, and selflessness over self-promotion. If Americans had trouble understanding what I was getting at, what was a Chinese audience going to think?

When the day of my talk arrived, I got up in front of a packed ballroom in the St. Regis Hotel in Shenzhen to address the gathered business owners who filled every seat. Bolstered by a talented interpreter, my confidence grew as I watched audience members scribbling furiously in their notebooks. With each point I made, people nodded and leaned forward.

Then, at the end of my allotted 45 minutes, I closed with a statement that I had used a number of times before.

"The thing about hype," I told them, "is that it's too powerful a tool to be left in the hands of the bad guys alone. That's why I've made it my life's work to teach it to incredible entrepreneurs like you, people who are creating products and services that are designed to make the world better. If I can do my part in getting us to a place where the best people making the best stuff are armed with the strategies to most effectively—and ethically—attract attention to what they're doing, I will have had a life worth living."

The crowd exploded—a full-fledged standing ovation.

As I basked in the applause, happy and stunned, I happened to lock eyes with a young woman in the front row.

She was crying.

When it comes to entrepreneurship, China still exists on the margins—at least in regard to how the people see themselves.

Every conversation I had during my trip made it clear that even the most successful Chinese entrepreneurs have an inferiority complex. They still see themselves as running behind the Western world, especially the US.

Despite China's trending toward free enterprise over the last couple of decades, overt self-promotion still stands in complete contrast to thousands of years of Chinese cultural history. Even now, dedicating your life to the pursuit of the kind of nonconformity and individualistic decision-making it takes to be an entrepreneur makes you a bit of a misfit.

The American businesspeople in my audience at home had the societal structure and support that put them directly in the center of the mainstream. They had the luxury of speaking about how the world should be.

On the other hand, the Chinese entrepreneurs I spoke to have had to see the world as it really is. It was what made them successful in a culture that didn't naturally support their aspirations. So to hear someone like me come out and tell them that it was not just all right, but flat-out desirable, to view the world the way they always had, and to do what they had always done, really touched them. It touched me too. The experience made me realize that as far as life's work goes, this is pretty good stuff.

Imagine a world where the best ideas, the greatest products, the most interesting art, and the most meaningful causes don't get swallowed up and forgotten. Imagine a world where the best people understand the best methods for getting attention and for building the biggest, most energetic audiences.

This is what hype can give us.

NOW FOR SOME RANDOM TIDBITS

Since this is my epilogue, I get to use it however I want to. And the way I want to use the rest of it is to give you a few additional closing tips and techniques that didn't fit in any of the other chapters.

All of what follows is a set of metastrategies for the advanced hype artist. You should keep all of them in mind while you practice any of the hype strategies we've discussed, alone or in combination.

Engage in Relentless Experimentation

In reading about the previous strategies, one might get the impression that as long as you follow the strategies as laid out, you'll get the same results as the masters I got them from.

Not exactly.

While there are universal principles of hype, details matter a lot, as they do in any other area of human interaction. When people apply the same strategies the same way, regardless of time period or specific circumstances, it always falls short in the long run.

To truly learn something—anything—it must be practiced in the arena of real life. Book learning is important, but it is never sufficient. Some degree of trial and error will always be necessary to adapt what you know in the abstract to the specifics of your time, your personality, and your audience.

When it comes to sales, people skip this step all the time. They read every sales book and take every sales course and then bet their entire fortunes on the step-by-step system they memorized. Then they're shocked when it doesn't work out.

Remember our old friends Mystery and Style? Like you, they were students of human psychology. They began their road to becoming master seducers by educating themselves through books, audio programs, and seminars. But they quickly realized that while this education was essential to their success, it wasn't enough.

Mystery and Style became successful with women because they took the theory into the bars and clubs. They approached hundreds of women and got rejected hundreds of times. They said hundreds of stupid things. But every time they did so, they studied the data and adjusted their approach. If you want to become a master of hype, you must do the same.

Become a Lifelong Student of Hype

You should be convinced by now that throughout the course of history, certain people have had an uncanny ability to get large numbers of other people to believe what they wanted them to believe and do what they wanted them to do. These people have gone by many names and plied many trades. Magicians. Prophets. Soothsayers. Spiritualists. Shamans. Gurus. Consultants.

Hype artists, every one of them.

This book should be nothing more than a starting point for you. If you're truly serious about building an audience for whatever you are selling that will stick with you wherever you go and whatever you do, you need to continue to seek out new hype artists to learn from.

Put down the marketing and sales books. Forget about the Build-a-Nine-Figure-Online-Business courses. Instead, seek out and study the real masters. When you learn from the true artists of mass manipulation, then you can build the business or company or following or movement you want and name your price for whatever it is you're selling.

Engage in Benevolent Mischief (Not Harmful Hucksterism)

While the core principles of hype hold constant whether they are being deployed by the most devious of demagogues or the most altruistic of activists, the actual content on whose behalf they are being applied really does make all the difference.

We've talked about managers like Shep Gordon who used hype to pack an arena for Alice Cooper—a band whose songs were once praised by Bob Dylan. When Thomas Edison used hype to bring attention to his work, the world got electric light, recorded sound, and motion pictures. Richard Branson uses hype to deliver top-flight entertainment and luxury travel experiences at afford-able prices.

On the other hand, Bernie Madoff used hype to get some of the world's wealthiest and most powerful people to invest in his Ponzi scheme for years. Theranos founder Elizabeth Holmes hyped her way into a multibillion-dollar valuation without ever having created a working product. And Fyre Festival founder Billy McFarland used it to sell 5,000 tickets at an average of a thousand dollars a pop to an event that was plagued by filth and chaos.

If you have an awesome product or service but its newness and your lack of visibility are keeping you from success, faking it until you make it makes sense as a strategy. But if you haven't created anything valuable, work on that first. Learn your craft. Become an expert. Build something solid. Once you're confident that you'll have the ability to deliver on your promises, a little bit of hype won't hurt you—or your customers. In fact, it might add the splash of color and excitement people crave.

Whichever way you end up using this powerful set of strat-egies drawn from the assorted cult leaders, propagandists, and hucksters we've spent time with, it is my sincerest wish that you will apply them to projects and causes that improve people's lives.

While there are already plenty of people who understand how to use the ideas in this book to sell garbage, I have a lot of hope. If these strategies can be used to push that which deceives and degrades, imagine what can happen if more and more people apply them to work that enhances and enriches. Hype artists may see the world as it really is, but the best of them use that knowledge to make it better. Now that you know their secrets, I hope you'll join their ranks.

BIBLIOGRAPHY

BOOKS

Anand, Bharat. *The Content Trap: A Strategist's Guide to Digital Change*. New York: Random House, 2016.

Artaud, Antonin. *The Theater and Its Double*. New York: Grove Press, 1958.

Barabási, Albert-László. *The Formula: The Universal Laws of Success*. New York: Little, Brown and Company, 2018.

Bernays, Edward. *Crystallizing Public Opinion*. New York: Ig Publishing, 1923.

Bernays, Edward. *Propaganda*. New York: Ig Publishing, 1928.

Bockris, Victor. *Warhol: The Biography*. London: Da Capo Press, 1997.

Branson, Richard. *Losing My Virginity: How I Survived, Had Fun, and Made a Fortune Doing Business My Way.* New York: Crown Publishing, 1998.

Brock, Pope. *Charlatan: America's Most Dangerous Huckster, the Man Who Pursued Him, and the Age of Flimflam.* New York: Three Rivers Press, 2009.

Butler, E. M. *The Myth of the Magus.* Cambridge: Cambridge University Press, 1948.

Butterfield, Steve. *Amway: The Cult of Free Enterprise.* Boston: South End Press, 1985.

Carnegie, Dale. *How to Win Friends and Influence People.* New York: Simon & Schuster, 1936.

Chuang Tzu (trans. Martin Palmer). *The Book of Chuang Tzu.* New York: Penguin, 2006.

Daichendt, James G. *Shepard Fairey Inc.: Artist/Professional/ Vandal.* San Francisco: Cameron and Co., 2014.

Ecko, Marc. *Unlabel: Selling You Without Selling Out.* New York: Touchstone, 2013.

Ehrenreich, Barbara. *Bright-Sided: How Positive Thinking Is Undermining America.* New York: Henry Holt and Company, 2009.

Emmons, Henry. *The Chemistry of Calm.* New York: Atria, 2015.

Evanzz, Karl. *The Messenger: The Rise and Fall of Elijah Muhammad.* New York: Vintage, 1999.

Ferriss, Tim. *The 4-Hour Workweek: Escape 9–5, Live Anywhere, and Join the New Rich.* New York: Harmony, 2007.

Fried, Jason, and Hansson, David Heinemeier. *Rework.* New York: Crown Business, 2010.

Goldsmith, Barbara. *Other Powers: The Age of Suffrage, Spiritualism and the Scandalous Victoria Woodhull.* New York: Knopf, 1998.

Gordon, Mel. *Theatre of Fear and Horror: The Grisly Spectacle of the Grand Guignol of Paris 1897–1962.* Port Townsend, WA: Feral House, 2016.

Gordon, Shep. *They Call Me Supermensch: A Backstage Pass to the Amazing Worlds of Film, Food, and Rock 'n' Roll.* New York: HarperCollins, 2016.

Greene, Robert. *The Art of Seduction.* New York: Penguin, 2001.

Guinn, Jeff. *Manson: The Life and Times of Charles Manson.* New York: Simon & Schuster, 2013.

Heller, Anne C. *Ayn Rand and the World She Made.* New York: Anchor Books, 2009.

Hoffer, Eric. *The True Believer: Thoughts on the Nature of Mass Movements.* New York: Harper & Row, 1951.

Holiday, Ryan. *Trust Me, I'm Lying: Confessions of a Media Manipulator.* New York: Portfolio/Penguin, 2012.

Hubbard, L. Ron. *Dianetics: The Modern Science of Mental Health.* Los Angeles: Bridge Publications, 2007.

Hyde, Lewis. *Trickster Makes This World: Mischief, Myth, and Art.* New York: Farrar, Straus and Giroux, 1998.

Johnson, Paul. *Intellectuals: From Marx and Tolstoy to Sartre and Chomsky.* New York: HarperCollins, 1988.

Lakoff, George. *Don't Think of an Elephant! Know Your Values and Frame the Debate.* White River Junction, VT: Chelsea Green Publishing, 2004.

Le Bon, Gustave. *The Crowd: A Study of the Popular Mind.* London: T. Fisher Unwin, 1896.

Macknik, Stephen L., and Martinez-Conde, Susana. *Slights of Mind: What the Neuroscience of Magic Reveals About Our Everyday Deceptions.* New York: Henry Holt and Company, 2010.

McLeod, Kembrew. *Pranksters: Making Mischief in the Modern World.* New York: New York University Press, 2014.

McNeil, Legs, and McCain, Gillian. *Please Kill Me: The Uncensored Oral History of Punk.* New York: Penguin Books, 1997.

Miller, James. *Flowers in the Dustbin: The Rise of Rock and Roll, 1947–1977.* New York: Simon & Schuster, 1999.

Mlodinow, Leonard. *Subliminal: How Your Unconscious Mind Rules Your Behavior.* New York: Vintage Books, 2012.

Oldham, Andrew Loog. *Stoned: A Memoir of London in the 1960s.* New York: St. Martin's Press, 2000.

Orrmont, Arthur. *Love Cults and Faith Healers.* New York: Ballantine Books, 1961.

Pinker, Steven. *The Language Instinct.* New York: William Morrow and Company.

Pratkanis, Anthony, and Aronson, Elliot. *Age of Propaganda: The Everyday Use and Abuse of Persuasion.* New York: Henry Holt and Company, 1992.

Ries, Laura. *Battlecry: Winning the Battle for the Mind with a Slogan That Kills.* Self-published, 2015.

Slingerland, Edward. *Trying Not to Try: The Art and Science of Spontaneity.* New York: Random House, 2014.

Stewart, Matthew. *The Management Myth: Debunking Modern Business Philosophy.* New York: W. W. Norton & Company, 2009.

Strauss, Neil. *The Game: Penetrating the Secret Society of Pickup Artists.* New York: Dey Street Books, 2005.

Stross, Randall. *The Wizard of Menlo Park: How Thomas Alva Edison Invented the Modern World.* New York: Three Rivers Press, 2007.

Taylor, Kathleen: *Brainwashing: The Science of Thought Control.* Oxford: Oxford University Press, 2004.

Tolokonnikova, Nadya. *Read & Riot: A Pussy Riot Guide to Activism.* New York: HarperCollins, 2018.

Twain, Mark. *The Adventures of Tom Sawyer.* New York: Penguin Books, 1883.

Washington, Peter. *Madame Blavatsky's Baboon: A History of the Mystics, Mediums, and Misfits Who Brought Spiritualism to America.* New York: Schocken Books, 1993.

Weiner-Davis, Michele. *The Divorce Remedy: The Proven 7-Step Program for Saving Your Marriage.* New York: Simon & Schuster, 2002.

Wilson, A. N. *Paul: The Mind of the Apostle.* New York: W. W. Norton & Company, 1997.

Wright, Lawrence. *Going Clear: Scientology, Hollywood, and the Prison of Belief.* New York: Vintage Books, 2013.

Wu, Tim. *The Attention Merchants: The Epic Scramble to Get Inside Our Heads.* New York: Alfred A. Knopf, 2016.

Xygalatas, Dimitris. "Fire-Walking and the Brain: The Physiology of High-Arousal Rituals." In Bulbulia, J., Sosis, R., Harris, E., Genet, R., Genet, C., and Wyman K. (eds.), *Evolution of Religion: Studies, Theories, and Critiques.* Santa Margarita, CA: Collins Foundation Press, 2008.

ARTICLES, PAPERS, VIDEOS, PODCASTS, LECTURES

Abbott, Karen. "The Fox Sisters and the Rap on Spiritualism." *Smithsonian Magazine*, October 30, 2012.

Alicke, Mark D., and Ransom, Michael R. "It's a Miracle: Separating the Miraculous from the Mundane." *Archive for the Psychology of Religion*, 2012.

Buck, Stephanie. "The Weird, Rabid History of the Cabbage Patch Craze." *Timeline*, December 15, 2016.

Childers, Thomas. "German Political Culture." Class lecture, History 430: The Third Reich, University of Pennsylvania, Philadelphia, 1999.

"Chrissie Hynde." *WTF with Marc Maron* podcast. Episode 556. December 4, 2014.

"Drama Elements." *BBC Bite Size*, 2020.

Elliot, Bryan. "Why Gary Vaynerchuk Tells It Like It Is." Video. Mashable, January 25, 2012.

Grant, Adam. "Say Goodbye to MBTI, the Fad That Won't Die." LinkedIn, September 17, 2013.

Holiday, Ryan. "I Helped Create the Milo Trolling Playbook. You Should Stop Playing Right into It." *New York Observer*, February 7, 2017.

"Jesus, CEO." *The Economist*, December 20, 2005.

Marean, Curtis W. "How *Homo Sapiens* Became the Ultimate Invasive Species." *Scientific American*, July 14, 2015.

Menand, Louis. "What Personality Tests Really Deliver." *The New Yorker*, September 3. 2018.

"The Mormons." *American Experience, Frontline.* https://www.pbs.org/mormons/faqs/mission.html.

Rhode, Jason. "The Sudden, Shocking Fall of Nate Silver." *Paste*, July 13, 2016.

Sinek, Simon. "Millennials in the Workplace." https://www.youtube.com/watch?v=hER0Qp6QJNU.

Stromberg, Joseph, and Caswell, Estelle. "Why the Myers-Briggs Test Is Totally Meaningless." Vox, October 8, 2015.

Wohlsen, Marcus. "I Just Want Nate Silver to Tell Me It's All Going to Be Fine." *Wired.* October 16, 2016.

The best hype artists never stop learning. Neither should you.

If you would like me to send you my recommendations of additional books about propaganda, cult tactics, blatant self-promotion, and various other forms of mischief making, visit hypereads.com/list.

INDEX

Antisocial personality disorder
(APD), 162
APA (American Psychological
Association), 97
Apollo (Greek god), 55–56
Appreciation, 16–17, 20–21
Arbitrage, psychological, 106–108
Arlene's Grocery (New York, N.Y.),
30
Aronson, Elliot, 7, 27, 38, 155–156
Arousal, rituals causing, 135–138
The Art of Seduction (Greene), 66
Assessment tools, developing,
150–151
Athens, ancient, 126
Atlantic crossing, in hot-air
balloon, 74–76
Attention, xx, 63–66
Audience, cultivating, 24–25
Authority, 98, 104

BabyLand General, 130
Bacon, 13–15
Baldr the Bright (Norse god), 63
Baldwin, Alec, 144
Barabási, Albert-László, 62
Basecamp, 128–129
"Battle Hymn of the Republic"
(song), 49
The Beatles, 60
Beecher, Henry Ward, 45
Beech-Nut, 14
Behavior:
formulas and statistics on,
100–102
slogans about, 119
Behavioral engineering, 101–102
Beliefs:
about change, 50–53
building communities around,
149–151

challenging accepted, 61, 126
and dealing with uncertainty,
141–145
holding contradictory, 157
setting down your, 141–152
writing books about, 145–148
Benevolent mischief, 57, 175–177
Bernays, Edward, 13–15, 21, 25
"Bibles," writing, 145–148
Biden, Hunter, 6
Billboard (magazine), 121
Billboards, defacing, 66–68
Bin, Qingchi "C Bin," 106–108, 171
Binaca, 132
Bismarck, Otto von, 8–9, 11
Blame, 161
Blavatsky, "Madame" Helena, 76,
145–147
BMW, 116
Bolshevik Revolution, 77, 112
Book in Box, 24–25
Book of Doctrine and Covenants,
45
Books, writing, 145–148
Boredom, 127–128
Boston University, 106
Bowie, David, 20–21, 29, 30
Brand positioning, 115
Brand recognition, 132
Branson, Richard, xxi, 74–77, 176
Breakfast, eating habits at, 13–15
Brecht, Bertolt, 27–30
Brehm, Jack, 51
Brehm, Sharon, 51
Briggs, Katharine Cook, 150–151
Bright-Sided (Ehrenreich), 98
Brinkley, "Dr." John R., xxi, 34
Brown, Nick, 99
Buffett, Warren, 50–51
Burger King, 115
Burlington, Vt., 38

ABOUT THE AUTHOR

Michael F. Schein is the founder and president of MicroFame Media, a marketing agency that specializes in making idea-based companies famous in their industries. Some of his clients have included eBay, Magento, The Medici Group, University of Pennsylvania, Gordon College, University of California Irvine, United Methodist Publishing House, Ricoh, LinkedIn, and Citrix. His writing has appeared in *Fortune, Forbes, Inc., Psychology Today,* and *Huffington Post,* and he is a speaker for international audiences spanning from the northeastern United States to the southeastern coast of China. He is also the creator of the popular Hype Book Club, which provides regular recommendations of books about hype artists and hype strategies. You can download these recommendations for yourself by visiting hypereads.com/list.